Good Old-Fashioned Puddings

Good Old-Fashioned Puddings

Sara Paston-Williams

NATIONAL TRUST BOOKS

First published in Great Britain in 1983 by
David & Charles under the title *The National Trust Book of Traditional Puddings*
New edition published in 2002 by
National Trust Enterprises Limited

This edition published in the United Kingdom in 2008 for Index Books Ltd by
National Trust Books
10 Southcombe Street
London W14 0RA

An imprint of Anova Books Ltd

ISBN-13 9781905400508

A CIP catalogue record for this book is available from the British Library.

15 14 13 12 11 10 09 08
10 9 8 7 6 5 4 3 2 1

Reproduction by Spectrum Colour Ltd, England
Printed and bound by CT Printing Ltd, China

Design by Lee-May Lim
Photography by Tara Fisher
Home Economy by Jane Suthering

Contents

Introduction

Blessed be he that invented pudding! For it is manna that hits the palates of all sortes of people, better even than that of the wilderness. Ah! what an excellent thing is an English pudding! To come in pudding-time is as much as to say to come in the most lucky moment in the world.

This was written by a Monsieur Misson de Valbourg, a French visitor to Britain in 1690. Another visitor, an Italian, around the same time wrote home saying 'English pies and puddings are literally stuffed with dried fruits and no-one who has not seen it with his own eyes could possibly believe what an incredible number of such pies and puddings the average Englishman is capable of eating!'

The British tradition for delicious puddings is centuries old. Puddings – pies, trifles, fools, flummeries, betties and tarts – have all been served regularly since medieval times. From the earliest recipes, through elaborate Elizabethan and Stuart confections to the elegant 18th- and substantial 19th-century puddings, a tradition has evolved which is an integral part of Britain's culinary heritage.

Almost all British puddings (and here, as in the rest of the book, I am using the word to describe any dish served at the sweet course) have descended from two medieval dishes: the early cereal 'pottage', which was a kind of porridge with honey, wild fruits, shredded meat or fish added to make it more palatable, and 'frumenty', a milk pudding made from wheat or barley and eaten with milk and honey on festive occasions. Originally, puddings such as brightly coloured spiced jellies, flummeries, syllabubs, various tarts, custards, junkets and fruit dishes formed part of a second or third course of a meal, served alongside chicken and fish dishes. A typical second course might consist of veal, sweetbreads, lobster, apricot tart and, in the middle of the table, a pyramid of syllabubs and jellies. In Tudor and Stuart times a special course of sweetmeats known as a 'banquet' became fashionable among the rich.

The enormous variety of puddings and the rapidity with which they were developed in the 17th and 18th centuries, as sugar became cheaper and more available to everyone, show that they filled a real need in the British people's diet – rich in fat and carbohydrates to keep out the cold, and in sugar and fruit to build up energy. The puddings of country folk were often made from meal of cheaper local grains such as oats and barley rather than wheat, but they were just as satisfying.

British cooking has always been influenced by its monarchs and our puddings are no exception. Elizabeth I received annually 'a great pye of quinces, oringed' from her master of the pastry at New Year celebrations. George I was known as 'Pudding George' and is probably the Georgie Porgie mentioned in the well-known nursery rhyme. He, followed by George II and III, loved fattening, suety boiled puddings and dumplings which were devoured all over the kingdom. It was also quite common to see plum duffs and currant dumplings being sold in the streets of London for a halfpenny each.

With the French Revolution came a great transformation in British cooking. Many French chefs fled to Britain and a change of fashion in court circles resulted in the vogue for employing them. Antonin Carême, who worked for the Emperor Napoleon, was lured to Britain to work for the Prince Regent. Queen Victoria employed a number of French chefs, the most famous being Francatelli, who created puddings which we still know – Queen's Pudding, Her Majesty's Pudding, Empress Pudding and Albert Pudding. This fashion was soon copied by a growing and increasingly prosperous middle class who, socially aspiring, encouraged their cooks to make French dishes or, failing that, simply to give French names to traditional British ones. Many of the most delicious and subtle puddings of Georgian times were temporarily forgotten, giving way to rather heavy nursery-style puddings influenced by the German taste of Prince Albert.

Growing literacy had a tremendous influence on cookery. It allowed people, especially women, to write down their favourite recipes, including regional dishes. Many of the traditional pudding recipes were preserved in rural areas, particularly in the large country houses. In towns, speciality restaurants, gentlemen's clubs and grill rooms of the more exclusive hotels continued to serve truly British puddings, so that many recipes have survived, although not always in their original form. In recent years, British food has enjoyed a well-deserved revival, with more and more hotels and restaurants serving our great national dishes and regional specialities. Puddings are a great attraction. Although some are inclined to be rich and fattening, they are homely and delicious and make a lovely treat. Despite our modern obsession with calories, 'pudding-time' still brings murmurs of delight from guests as they tuck into a syrup sponge or plum crumble. Our traditional puddings are glorious – rich and indulgent and comforting. Naughty? Yes, but oh so nice!

Note:
If you want to be a little less indulgent, yoghurt and crème fraîche can be used instead of cream in most recipes, or half and half.

Vegetarian alternatives:
Vegetarian suet and the vegetarian equivalent of lard can be used wherever a recipe includes suet or lard. In fact, I prefer to use vegetarian suet as it gives a lighter finish. Vegetarian setting agents can also be used in place of gelatine, however you must follow the manufacturer's instructions closely.

Conversions

Weight	Liquid measure	Length	Temperature
15g (½oz)	15ml (½fl oz)	5mm (¼in)	110°C, 225°F, gas mark ¼
25g (1oz)	30ml (lfl oz)	1cm (½in)	120°C, 250°F, gas mark ½
40g (1½oz)	50ml (2fl oz)	1.5cm (⅝in)	140°C, 275°F, gas mark 1
55g (2oz)	75ml (2½fl oz)	2cm (¾in)	150°C, 300°F, gas mark 2
70g (2½oz)	125ml (4fl oz)	2.5cm (1in)	160°C, 325°F, gas mark 3
85g (3oz)	100ml (3½fl oz)	5cm (2in)	180°C, 350°F, gas mark 4
100g (3½oz)	150ml (5fl oz or ¼ pint)	7cm (2¾in)	190°C, 375°F, gas mark 5
115g (4oz)	200ml (7fl oz or ⅓ pint)	9cm (3½in)	200°C, 400°F, gas mark 6
125g (4½oz)	250ml (9fl oz)	10cm (4in)	220°C, 425°F, gas mark 7
140g (5oz)	300ml (10fl oz or ½ pint)	13cm (5in)	230°C, 450°F, gas mark 8
150g (5½oz)	350ml (12fl oz)	15cm (6in)	240°C, 475°F, gas mark 9
175g (6oz)	400ml (14fl oz)	18cm (7in)	
200g (7oz)	425ml (15fl oz or ¾ pint)	20cm (8in)	
225g (8oz)	500ml (18fl oz)	23cm (9in)	
250g (9oz)	600ml (20fl oz or l pint)	25cm (10in)	
300g (10½oz)		28cm (11in)	
350g (12oz)		30cm (12in)	
375g (13oz)			
400g (14oz)			
425g (15oz)			
450g (1lb)			
675g (1½lb)			
900g (2lb)			

These approximate conversions are used throughout this book.

American Equivalents

<table>
<tr><td colspan="3">Dry measures</td></tr>
<tr><td>1 US cup</td><td>50g (1¾oz)</td><td>breadcrumbs; cake crumbs</td></tr>
<tr><td>1 US cup</td><td>85g (3oz)</td><td>porridge or rolled oats</td></tr>
<tr><td>1 US cup</td><td>90g (3¼oz)</td><td>ground almonds; shredded coconut</td></tr>
<tr><td>1 US cup</td><td>100g (3½oz)</td><td>roughly chopped walnuts and other nuts; icing sugar; cocoa; drinking chocolate; flaked almonds; grated Cheddar cheese</td></tr>
<tr><td>1 US cup</td><td>150g (5½oz)</td><td>white flour; currants; rice flour; muesli; cornflour; chopped dates</td></tr>
<tr><td>1 US cup</td><td>175g (6oz)</td><td>wholemeal flour; oatmeal; raisins; sultanas; dried apricots; mixed candied peel</td></tr>
<tr><td>1 US cup</td><td>200g (7oz)</td><td>caster sugar; soft brown sugar; demerara sugar; rice; glacé cherries; semolina; chopped figs or plums</td></tr>
<tr><td>1 US cup</td><td>225g (8oz)</td><td>granulated sugar; curd cheese; cream cheese</td></tr>
<tr><td>1 US cup</td><td>300g (10½oz)</td><td>mincemeat; marmalade; jam</td></tr>
<tr><td>1 US cup</td><td>350g (12oz)</td><td>golden syrup; black treacle</td></tr>
</table>

Liquid measures

⅛ US cup	30ml (1fl oz)
¼ US cup	50ml (2fl oz)
½ US cup	125ml (4fl oz)
1 US cup	250ml (9fl oz)
1¼ US cups	300ml (10fl oz)
1¾ US cups	425ml (15fl oz)
2 US cups	500ml (18fl oz)
2½ US cups	600ml (20fl oz)

Measures for fats

¼ stick	25g (1oz)
1 stick (½ US cup)	100g (3½oz)

Baked Puddings

The discovery of the pudding cloth in the 17th century was a vital factor in the great expansion of pudding eating, but Elizabethan cooks had already devised another method of cooking puddings that avoided boiling in animal guts. The pudding mixture was baked in a 'coffyn' or 'platter' in the bread or side oven with a pastry crust over it like a tart. In the early part of the 17th century, a pudding baked in a pot was still known as a 'pudding pye'. Occasionally the baking dish was lined with a thin sheet of pastry before the pudding mixture went into it, though this practice became more frequent in the 18th century. Sometimes the pastry was simply used to garnish the brim of the baking dish, to make it look elegant enough to be brought straight from the oven to the table.

Soon recipes for baked puddings were appearing regularly in cookery books. They were often based upon rich ingredients and this, together with the fact that an oven had to be heated for their baking, made them dishes for the wealthy rather than the poor. Fresh fruits in season were often substituted for the dried 'plums' in many recipes and baked puddings containing apples, apricots, Seville oranges, lemons and even carrots were common. Specially turned wooden baking dishes were sold in which the puddings could be cooked.

To give a crisp surface, a baked pudding mixture should be slightly softer than for a steamed or boiled pudding. If you use water instead of milk to soften the mixture, you will make a lighter pudding. To prevent jam, marmalade or chocolate from caramelizing during baking, stand your baking dish in a roasting tin half-filled with water.

Apple and Marmalade Charlotte

*Apple Charlotte was appearing in recipe books by the beginning of the 19th century, filled
with 'apple marmalade' (apples cooked in butter, sugar and spices, then beaten to a pulp).
This delicious recipe was given to me by the pastry chef at Christ's College, Cambridge, and
can be made in a charlotte mould, round cake tin, loaf tin or individual dariole moulds.*

225g (8oz) butter
115g (4oz) caster sugar
Slices of day-old white bread
600g (1lb 5oz) cooking apples

70g (2½oz) fresh white breadcrumbs
½ jar good-quality orange marmalade
1 tablespoon water

Serves 6

Melt the butter and brush the inside of your chosen mould, then coat with some of the caster sugar.
Remove the crusts from the slices of bread (their number will depend on your mould), then dip one
slice in the melted butter and place in the bottom of the mould.

Cut some slices of bread in half lengthways, then dip in butter and arrange overlapping each
other to line the sides of your mould, taking care not to leave any gaps for the fruit to seep through.
Peel, core and cut the apples into thick slices, and three parts cook in a little butter and sugar. Add
the breadcrumbs and about 1 tablespoon of the marmalade. Fill the centre of the mould with the
fruit mixture, pressing it down well and giving the mould a bang on the table to release any air.
Place a whole, crustless slice of bread, dipped in the remaining melted butter on the top of the apples
and bake in a preheated oven at 220°C, 425°F, gas mark 7, for 30–40 minutes or until brown.

Remove from the oven, and take off the piece of bread on the top. Trim around the edge of the
mould with a sharp knife, then turn out onto a warm serving plate. Melt the remaining marmalade
with the water, over a low heat, then pour over the charlotte. Serve hot with Vanilla Custard Sauce or
Vanilla Ice Cream (see pages 29 and 59).

Variation

Crispy Pear Charlotte

This version has only a topping of buttery bread, and is made in a 1.2 litre (2 pint) ovenproof dish.
Peel, core and slice 450g (1lb) pears. Put half in the buttered dish. Sprinkle with 2 tablespoons soft
brown sugar, and spread with 2 tablespoons apricot jam. Cover with remaining pears and another 2
tablespoons sugar and apricot jam. Remove crusts from 6 slices white bread and cut each into 4
triangles. Dip into 115g (4oz) melted butter and arrange on top of pears. Sprinkle with another
tablespoon of sugar, then bake at 190°C, 375°F, gas mark 5 for 30–40 minutes until crisp and golden.

Apple Dappy

A traditional Victorian recipe from the West Country, where apples were grown in vast quantities for eating and for cider.

FOR THE LEMON SYRUP
1 large lemon
1 tablespoon golden syrup
15g (½oz) butter
115g (4oz) caster sugar
200ml (7fl oz) water

FOR THE PUDDING
225g (8oz) self-raising flour
1 level teaspoon baking powder
55g (2oz) butter, cut in small pieces
150ml (¼ pint) milk
450g (1lb) cooking apples
1 tablespoon demerara sugar
¼ teaspoon ground cinnamon or allspice

Serves 4–6

Preheat the oven to 190°C, 375°F, gas mark 5.

To make the lemon syrup, peel the lemon as thinly as possible and squeeze out the juice. Place the lemon rind, juice and all the other ingredients, into a pan and heat gently, stirring until the sugar is dissolved. Leave to stand until needed.

Sieve the flour and baking powder into a large mixing bowl and rub in the butter until the mixture resembles breadcrumbs. Mix to a dough with the milk, then roll out on a floured board to about 20cm (8in) square and approximately 5mm (¼in) thick.

Peel, core and chop the apples, then spread on the pastry. Sprinkle with the sugar and spice and roll up like a Swiss roll. Cut into 2.5cm (1in) slices and arrange in a buttered 1.2 litre (2 pint) ovenproof dish.

Strain the lemon rind from the prepared syrup and pour over the pudding. Bake for about 30 minutes, or until puffed up and golden. Serve hot with Vanilla Custard Sauce (see page 29) or clotted cream.

Nottingham Pudding

Also known as Apple-In-and-Out, this pudding is a combination of apple and batter, dating back to medieval days when dried fruits, spices and candied peel were put in a batter pudding and served with joints of meat. This tradition has continued in the north of England, where any leftovers are served after the meal with melted butter and treacle, lemon juice and sugar or warmed honey and cinnamon.

115g (4oz) plain flour
Pinch of salt
1 large egg
150ml (¼ pint) full-cream milk
150ml (¼ pint) water
450g (1lb) cooking apples

40g (1½oz) butter
Grated rind of ½ lemon
½ teaspoon ground cinnamon
70g (2½oz) soft brown sugar
40g (1½oz) margarine

Serves 4–6

Sieve flour and salt together into a basin and make a well in the centre. Break the egg into the well and stir to mix with the flour. Gradually add half the milk and water, beating well with a wooden spoon until batter is smooth and creamy. Add remaining liquid, beating with a rotary or electric whisk to keep batter smooth and light. Leave to stand in a cool place for about 30 minutes.

Peel, core and slice the apples. Melt the butter in a heavy frying pan, add the apples, lemon rind, cinnamon and sugar, cover and cook gently until the apples are just tender.

Put the margarine in a 19cm (7½in) square baking tin and heat near the top of a preheated oven at 220°C, 425°F, gas mark 7 until the fat is smoking. Remove from the oven and carefully add the apple mixture and pour the batter over. Return to the oven for about 20 minutes, then reduce temperature to 190°C, 375°F, gas mark 5 for a further 20–25 minutes or until batter is firm and golden brown (this batter pudding will not rise as much as a Yorkshire pudding, because of the fruit it contains).

Variation

Sweet Batter Pudding

Leave out the apples and bake a plain batter. Serve immediately with melted golden syrup or honey poured over the pudding, and sprinkled with caster sugar, or serve with Jam, Marmalade or Syrup Sauce (see pages 92, 155 and 156). You can vary this recipe by adding 50g (1¾oz) raisins or sultanas.

Mother Eve's Pudding

Traditionally made with tempting apples under a sponge topping, hence the name! However, you can use any fruit and the flavourings can be varied accordingly by adding spices or orange rind. The Georgian recipe for this pudding was made with suet and included currants as well as the apples. It was also boiled rather than baked.

600g (1lb 5oz) cooking apples
85g (3oz) caster sugar
Grated rind of 1 lemon
2 cloves
1 tablespoon water
115g (4oz) salted butter

115g (4oz) caster sugar
2 eggs
¼ teaspoon vanilla extract
115g (4oz) self-raising flour
1 tablespoon warm water
Caster sugar for dredging

Serves 6

Butter a 1.2 litre (2 pint) ovenproof dish. Peel, core and slice apples thinly and place in a heavy saucepan with sugar, lemon rind, cloves and water. Heat over gentle heat for a few minutes until just tender. Turn into prepared dish and leave to cool.

Cream butter and sugar together in a mixing bowl until pale and fluffy. Beat eggs and add gradually to creamed mixture, beating well after each addition. Beat in the vanilla essence, and gently fold sieved flour into creamed mixture. Stir in warm water to make a soft dropping consistency and spread evenly over apples.

Bake in the centre of a preheated oven at 190°C, 375°F, gas mark 5 for about 45minutes, or until well risen and golden brown (test with a fine skewer which should come out clean). Serve hot or cold, dredged with caster sugar and with Vanilla Custard or Lemon Sauce (see pages 29 and 133).

Variations

Apple and Almond Pudding
Substitute 115g (4oz) ground almonds for self-raising flour and continue as before. Serve hot or cold with pouring cream.

Apple and Marmalade Pudding
Make as before, but stir 2 rounded tablespoons Seville orange marmalade into the apple mixture, reducing the sugar to 25g (1oz) or less.

Apple Cobs

Also known as Bomdard'd Apples or Apple Dumplings. The original dumplings were boiled, but in this recipe they are baked. Use a really good quality cooking apple which will go soft and puffy when cooked. You can use shortcrust or puff pastry, instead of suet-crust pastry if you want a less rich pudding.

350g (12oz) self-raising flour
Pinch of salt
175g (6oz) suet
50g (1¾ oz) caster sugar
About 150ml (¼ pint) ice-cold water
6 medium Bramley apples

2 tablespoons mincemeat
6 cloves
Water or milk for brushing
1 egg white, beaten
3 tablespoons clotted cream
 (optional)

Serves 6

Sieve flour and salt together into a mixing bowl. Mix in suet and stir in half the sugar. Add just sufficient water to mix to a soft but not sticky dough. Turn out on to a lightly floured board and divide into 6 equal pieces. Roll out each piece thinly into a square large enough to encase an apple. Peel and core apples and place one in the centre of each pastry square. Fill each apple centre with mincemeat and top with a clove. Brush edge of each pastry square with a little water or milk, draw up corners to meet over the centre of each apple and press edges firmly together. Turn upside down, and place on a greased baking tray. Roll out the pastry trimmings to make small leaves to decorate the dumplings, then brush all over with the egg white and sprinkle with remaining sugar.

Bake in the centre of a preheated oven at 200°C, 400°F, gas mark 6 for 30 minutes or until golden brown. Remove from the oven and leave to stand for a few minutes on a warm serving dish. Cut a hole in the top of each dumpling and spoon in some clotted cream, or serve with Vanilla Custard Sauce (see page 29).

Variation

Apple and Blackberry Cobs
Fill the apples with blackberries (or other soft fruits), a little sugar and a knob of butter instead of mincemeat. Serve with Honey and Brandy Ice Cream (see page 55), Vanilla Custard Sauce (see page 29) or clotted cream.

Right: Apple Cobs

Apricot Amber Pudding

Traditionally, an Amber Pudding was made with apples and baked in a puff-pastry case. It is a very old-fashioned sweet dating back to the 18th century, and can be made with many other fruits such as apples, rhubarb, gooseberries, blackberries, blackcurrants or plums.

175g (6oz) shortcrust pastry
450g (1lb) fresh apricots
About 150g (5½oz) caster sugar
1 teaspoon lemon juice
25g (1oz) unsalted butter
2 eggs, separated
Pinch of salt
Crystallized apricot and angelica to decorate

Serves 6

Preheat the oven to 200°C, 400°C, gas mark 6, with a large baking sheet in the oven to warm up as well. Roll out the pastry thinly and use to line a buttered 20cm (8in) shallow ovenproof dish. Chill in the refrigerator for 30 minutes. Prick the base and line with baking paper and baking beans. Place in the oven on the hot baking sheet and bake blind for about 10 minutes, then remove the baking parchment and beans and cook for about another 10 minutes to dry out the inside without browning the pastry.

Meanwhile, wash and stone the apricots, then poach in a little water until tender. Rub the fruit through a plastic sieve, then sweeten with sugar to taste, adding the lemon juice. Stir in the butter, and beat in the egg yolks. Leave on one side to cool.

Pour the cooled apricot mixture into the cooked pastry case and cook for 20 minutes in the preheated oven at 200°C, 400°F, gas mark 6.

Whisk the egg whites with the salt until stiff, but not dry. Add 60g (2oz) caster sugar and whisk until stiff again. Fold in another 60g (2oz) sugar gently. Reduce the oven temperature to 180°C, 350°F, gas mark 4. Pile the meringue on top of the apricot mixture and spread out, making sure that it touches the edges of the pastry. Dredge with extra caster sugar and bake in the centre of the oven for 20 minutes, or until the meringue is crisp and very lightly browned.

Serve warm or cold with whipped cream and decorated with pieces of crystallized apricot and candied angelica, if you wish.

Left: Apricot Amber Pudding

Rich Bakewell Pudding

There are several 'original' recipes in Derbyshire for this famous pudding, but generally it is accepted that it was probably first made by a cook at the Rutland Arms in Bakewell two hundred years ago. Jane Austen was reputed to have stayed at this hotel while writing Pride and Prejudice.

The original recipe was made in a special oval tin 7.5cm (3in) deep and 15cm (6in) wide and had a thick layer of preserved fruit, such as peaches or apricots, and strips of candied citron or orange peel spread over the pastry. A custard made with eggs, butter and sugar and flavoured with what the Bakewellians call 'lemon brandy' (brandy flavoured with lemon rind) was poured on top of the preserved fruit and the pudding was baked. Ratafia or almond flavouring is more commonly used now, and flaky or rich shortcrust pastry can be used instead of shortcrust.

175g (6oz) shortcrust pastry
3 heaped tablespoons homemade or
   good-quality apricot jam
25g (1oz) candied peel, chopped
3 eggs
115g (4oz) caster sugar

115g (4oz) unsalted butter
½ teaspoon vanilla extract or
   ratafia flavouring
1 tablespoon brandy
115g (4oz) ground almonds
Sieved icing sugar for dredging

Serves 6

Roll out the pastry and use to line a buttered 20cm (8in) oval pie dish. Chill, then bake blind in the usual way (see Apricot Amber Pudding, page 17). Spread the jam evenly over the cooled pastry case and sprinkle with the peel.

Beat eggs and sugar together until pale and thick. Melt the butter and run into egg mixture. Beat together well. Stir in vanilla essence or ratafia and brandy. Fold in ground almonds. Pour mixture over jam and candied peel in the pastry case. Bake in the centre of the preheated oven at 180°C, 350°F, gas mark 4, for about 30 minutes or until filling is set and golden brown. Dredge with sieved icing sugar and serve hot, warm or cold with pouring cream.

Variation

Alderman's Pudding
A popular pudding in the south of England using apricot jam, but no candied peel or brandy.

Quantock Pudding

Batter puddings similar to the famous French Clafoutis used to be made in most fruit growing areas in Britain (see Cherry Batter, page 32). The Quantock or Somerset version used blackberries, but any soft fruits are suitable, as well as apples, pears, rhubarb, apricots and gooseberries.

50g (1¾oz) butter
55g (2oz) plain flour
4 medium eggs
115g (4oz) caster sugar
1 tablespoon Kirsch
1 vanilla pod, split in half lengthways and seeds scraped out
150ml (¼ pint) whipping cream
150ml (¼ pint) full-cream milk
450g (1lb) blackberries
Icing sugar to dust

Serves 4–6

Preheat the oven to 200°C, 400°F, gas mark 6. Using half the butter, liberally grease a shallow gratin, ovenproof baking dish or cast-iron frying pan with 1.2 litre (2 pint) capacity.

In a large bowl, whisk together the flour, eggs, sugar, Kirsch and seeds from the vanilla pod, until creamy, then stir in the cream and milk. Strain, if there are any lumps.

Place the buttered dish in the oven for a couple of minutes until very hot, then remove from the oven. Immediately pour in half of the batter, sprinkle the blackberries on top, then pour over the remaining batter. Dot remaining butter over the surface, then bake for 30 minutes, or until puffed up and golden brown and a skewer inserted into the mixture comes out completely clean.

Leave for at least 20 minutes before serving just warm and dusted with sieved icing sugar. Eat with lightly whipped cream.

Variation

Apple and Cinnamon Batter
Use 4 crisp dessert apples, peeled, cored and sliced thinly instead of the blackberries and include 1 level teaspoon cinnamon in the butter. Arrange the apple slices over the bottom of the buttered baking dish. Pour over the batter and bake as before.

Old-fashioned Bread Pud

In Plymouth, this very old pudding is called Nelson's Cake after the great man who was obviously a lover of it. It is also particularly popular in East Anglia, where Nelson was born. The original version would have been boiled but it is now more commonly baked. Individual bread puddings were fashionable in Georgian times – they were baked in buttered teacups.

225g (8oz) stale white or brown
    bread, with crusts removed
300ml (½ pint) milk
2 tablespoons brandy (optional)
50g (1¾oz) melted butter or suet
50g (1¾oz) soft brown sugar
2 level teaspoons mixed spice

1 egg, beaten
175g (6oz) mixed dried fruit
Grated rind of 1 lemon
Grated rind of ½ orange
Freshly grated nutmeg
Caster sugar for sprinkling

Serves 4

Break the bread into small pieces and put in a mixing bowl. Pour over the milk and brandy, if using, stir well and leave to soak for at least 30 minutes.

Add the melted butter or suet, sugar, spice and egg, then using a fork, beat out any lumps. Stir in the dried fruit and grated lemon and orange rind, then turn the mixture into a buttered 1.2 litre (2 pint) ovenproof dish. Grate nutmeg over the top.

Bake in a preheated oven at 180°C, 350°F, gas mark 4 for 1¼–1½ hours until nicely brown on top. Serve hot, sprinkled with caster sugar and with Vanilla Custard Sauce (see page 29) or with a cold Hard Sauce (see page 157).

Variation

Old-fashioned Iced Bread Pud
Make as before, but remove from the oven after 1 hour. Cover with meringue made from 2 egg whites and 115g (4oz) caster sugar. Put back in the oven and cook for a further 20 minutes, or until the meringue is crisp and lightly browned.

Gingerbread and Pear Upside-down Pudding

This was a popular pudding in Victorian days and looks very attractive. You can bake it in a round or square tin.

50g (1¾oz) butter
140g (5oz) soft brown sugar
3 firm pears
6 glacé cherries
6 walnut halves
115g (4oz) margarine
115g (4oz) black treacle
115g (4oz) golden syrup
225g (8oz) plain flour

¼ teaspoon salt
Pinch of ground cloves
2 teaspoons ground cinnamon
2 teaspoons ground ginger
¼ teaspoon grated nutmeg
1 level teaspoon bicarbonate of soda
150ml (¼ pint) warm full-cream milk
2 eggs

Serves 6

Line the bottom and sides of a 20cm (8in) round cake tin with buttered greaseproof paper. Melt the butter in a saucepan over gentle heat, add 70g (2½oz) brown sugar and stir for a few minutes until dissolved. Pour into the bottom of the tin. Peel, halve and core pears and put a glacé cherry in the centre of each pear half. Arrange pears in a circle cut-side down on the butter-and-sugar mixture with stalk ends facing the centre of the tin. Place walnut halves, cut-side down, between the pears.

Put margarine or lard, black treacle, golden syrup and remaining brown sugar in a saucepan and melt over a low heat. Sieve flour, salt and spices together into a mixing bowl. Dissolve soda in warm milk. Beat eggs and add to milk mixture when it has cooled a little. Make a well in the centre of the dry ingredients and pour in melted treacle mixture, followed by egg mixture. Stir together and beat thoroughly until a smooth batter is formed. Pour carefully over pears and walnuts. Bake in the centre of a preheated oven at 180°C, 350°F, gas mark 4 for 40–50 minutes or until well risen and firm (test with a skewer; it should come out clean). Remove from the oven and allow to shrink a little before turning out on to a warmed serving plate. Take great care when peeling off greaseproof paper.

Serve warm with cream or Vanilla Custard Sauce (see page 29).

Bread and Butter Pudding

Bread and butter pudding was in the recipe books by the 1720s, when it was made of freshly sliced and buttered bread with currants, beaten eggs and nutmeg. It was only in Victorian times that it became a means of putting stale bread to good use. Since then it has become a British institution and there are dozens of versions. Modern recipes sometimes add fresh or poached fruit, marmalade, apricot jam or chocolate and use brioche, fruit loaf, panettone and croissants. I love a bread and butter pudding with a high proportion of rich custard to bread, but you can add more bread and experiment as much as you like. The three important things to remember is that the custard should cover the bread initially, plenty of soaking time (overnight, if possible) should be allowed and the pudding should be cooked slowly in a bain-marie at a low temperature.

300ml (½ pint) full-cream or
   Jersey milk
300ml (½ pint) double cream
1 vanilla pod, split in half
   lengthways
4–6 slices cut from a good-quality
   white sandwich loaf
About 100g (3½oz) butter, softened

55g (2oz) sultanas, soaked in hot
   water until plump
25g (1oz) candied peel, chopped
   (optional)
3 large eggs
About 70g (2½oz) caster sugar
Freshly grated nutmeg
Icing sugar for dredging

Serves 6

Slowly heat the milk and cream with the vanilla pod including its scraped-out seeds, until boiling point is just reached. Take off the heat and leave to cool a little.

Remove the crusts from the bread and butter generously. Cut each slice into 4 triangles, then arrange, overlapping in the base of a well-buttered 1.5 litre (2¾ pint) ovenproof dish. Sprinkle with the soaked and drained sultanas and peel, if using.

Whisk the eggs with the sugar, then pour into a jug with the strained milk and cream mixture. Taste and add more sugar, if you wish. Whisk again, then carefully pour evenly over the bread, making sure that each triangle gets a good soaking (add more milk if the liquid doesn't cover the bread). Grate plenty of nutmeg over the surface, cover and leave to soak for at least 2 hours, preferably overnight, in the refrigerator. When ready to cook, place the dish in a roasting tin filled with hot water to the level of the top of the custard.

Bake in a preheated oven at 150°C, 300°F, gas mark 2 for 1–1¼ hours until just set and golden (after 30 minutes cooking time, dredge with icing sugar to crisp up the top). Rest for 20 minutes before serving. No extra cream is really necessary as the custard is very rich and delicious.

Chocolate Puddle Pudding

A firm family favourite, this pudding emerges from the oven with its own built-in sauce hidden under a layer of chocolate sponge. Its exact origin is vague although it has been around for years.

FOR THE PUDDING
115g (4oz) butter, softened
115g (4oz) soft light brown sugar
1 teaspoon vanilla extract
2 large eggs, beaten
85g (3oz) self-raising flour
25g (1oz) cocoa powder
A little milk

FOR THE SAUCE
85g (3oz) light brown sugar
25g (1oz) cocoa powder
300ml (½ pint) full-cream milk

Serves 4–6

Preheat the oven to 180°C, 350°F, gas mark 4. Cream the butter and sugar together until light and fluffy. Beat in the vanilla extract, then gradually beat in the eggs.

Sieve the flour and cocoa together, then fold into the creamed mixture. Mix in just enough milk to give a soft dropping consistency. Spoon into a buttered 1.2 litre (2 pint) ovenproof dish.

For the sauce, mix the sugar and cocoa together and gradually beat in the milk. Pour evenly over the pudding mixture and bake for 40–60 minutes, or until just set in the centre. (If the pudding is a bit too soft in the centre, the sauce will be thin when you cut into the pudding, but if you overcook so that the pudding is very firm in the centre, the sauce will disappear. The centre should spring back when you press it lightly, with your fingertips.) Leave to stand for 5 minutes, before serving with Vanilla Ice Cream (see page 59) or cream.

Damson Cobbler

This pudding presumably takes its name from the scone topping, which does look rather like cobblestones. You can either cut out dough into circles and place them round the edges of the dish, overlapping each other, or you can lay the dough over like a pie crust and cut it into squares – either way, it is a delicious and economical pudding. Many fruits can be used instead of damsons – plums, greengages, blackcurrants, blackberries, apples, rhubarb, bilberries and gooseberries. This particular recipe is made in Cumbria from local damsons.

900g (2lb) damsons
250g (9oz) caster sugar
150ml (¼ pint) water
225g (8oz) self-raising flour
Pinch of salt
55g (2oz) butter
1 egg
1–2 tablespoons milk
Granulated sugar for sprinkling

Serves 6

Wash damsons and cook slowly in a heavy saucepan with 225g (8oz) sugar and water until just tender. Remove the stones and turn into a buttered ovenproof dish. Leave to cool.

Sieve flour and salt together into a mixing bowl. Stir in remaining sugar and rub in the butter. Beat the egg and add to the mixture with enough milk to make a soft dough. Roll out on a lightly floured board to about 1cm (½in) thick. Cut out dough into rounds with a 5cm (2in) cutter and arrange in a ring around the edge of the dish of fruit with the rounds overlapping each other. Brush the scone topping with a little milk, and bake near the top of a preheated oven at 220°C, 425°F, gas mark 7 for 10 minutes. Reduce oven temperature to 190°C, 375°F, gas mark 5. Sprinkle the top generously with granulated sugar and bake for a further 5–10 minutes until well risen and golden brown.

Icky Sticky Toffee Sponge

A top favourite with most people, the original recipe for this pudding probably dates back to the 1930s. It was made famous in the 1960s by the late great Francis Coulson, chef and proprietor of the Sharrow Bay Country House Hotel in Ullswater, Cumbria.

FOR THE SPONGE
50g (1¾oz) butter
175g (6oz) granulated sugar
175g (6oz) dates, stoned and chopped
300ml (½ pint) water
1 teaspoon bicarbonate of soda
2 large eggs
175g (6oz) self-raising flour
A few drops of vanilla extract

FOR THE SAUCE
40g (1½oz) demerara sugar
1 tablespoon black treacle, golden syrup or honey
300ml (½ pint) double cream

Serves 6–8

To make the sponge, cream the butter and sugar together. Boil the chopped dates in the water for about 10 minutes or until soft, then add the bicarbonate of soda. Beat the eggs into the creamed mixture, followed by the sieved flour, dates, water and vanilla extract. Pour into a buttered 20cm (8in) round, loose-bottomed cake tin that is at least 7.5cm (3in) deep. Bake in a preheated oven at 180°C, 350°F, gas mark 4 for about 40 minutes, or until firm to the touch.

Meanwhile, make the sauce. Put the sugar and treacle in a pan and heat gently, stirring until the sugar has dissolved. Stir in the cream and bring to the boil. Remove from the heat and leave to stand until needed.

When the pudding is cooked, remove from the oven and leave for 5 minutes, then turn out onto a warm serving plate. Pour over the sauce. Put under the grill for a few minutes until the sauce bubbles, then serve with Vanilla Ice Cream (see page 59).

Jam Roly-poly

This popular pudding used to be boiled in a cloth or shirtsleeve, but baking gives the pastry a lovely crisp crust which is usually more popular with children. Mincemeat or golden syrup can be used instead of jam.

225g (8oz) self-raising flour
1 teaspoon mixed spice (optional)
Pinch of salt
115g (4oz) suet
About 8 tablespoons water

4–5 tablespoons good quality jam, warmed
Milk, for brushing
1 egg, beaten, to glaze
Caster sugar for sprinkling

Serves 4–6

Sieve flour, spice (if using) and salt together into a mixing bowl. Stir in suet and add just enough water to mix to a soft, but not sticky, dough. Turn out on to a lightly floured board and roll into a rectangle about 20 x 30cm (8 x 12in). Spread evenly with warm jam leaving a 1cm (½in) border all the way around. Fold this border over the jam and brush with milk. Roll up fairly loosely and press edges of dough together to seal them. Put in a lightly buttered roasting tin and brush with beaten egg. Sprinkle with caster sugar.

Bake in the centre of a preheated oven at 200°C, 400°F, gas mark 6, with the tin propped up so that the roly-poly rolls into one end, which helps to keep its shape. Cook for 35–40 minutes or until golden brown.

Serve warm, sprinkled with extra caster sugar and Vanilla Custard Sauce (see page 29).

Variations

Roly-poly with Blueberries
Make roly-poly as before, but fill with 300g (10½oz) fresh blueberries mixed with 1 tablespoon flour, 4 tablespoons caster sugar and juice of 1 lemon or lime. Try other seasonal soft fruits and serve with Vanilla Custard Sauce (see page 29), Vanilla Ice Cream (see page 59) or thick cream.

A Bedfordshire Clanger
Cook 450g (1lb) peeled, cored and thinly sliced cooking apples briefly with a little butter and 85g (3oz) caster sugar until tender. Leave to cool, then spread over pastry, roll up and cook as before.

Tewkesbury Saucer Batters

Saucers were used for baking small savoury and sweet pies and puddings years before they were used under teacups, and a few recipes still survive. This one comes from Gloucestershire and is for batter puddings baked in saucers. You can serve them filled with fresh soft fruit such as raspberries, blackberries, loganberries or strawberries. They make a very unusual pudding for a dinner party. The quantities given here will make 4 saucer batters which will be enough for 8 people, but if your guests or family have large appetites and can polish off a saucer batter each, you will have to make more batter!

225g (8oz) plain flour
¼ teaspoon salt
2 eggs, separated
600ml (1 pint) milk
700g (1lb 9oz) soft fruit
115–175g (4–6oz) caster sugar

Serves 4–8

Sieve flour and salt together into a mixing bowl. Make a well in the centre and put in egg yolks. Beat in egg yolks gradually, adding milk a little at a time and beating continuously until the mixture becomes a smooth creamy batter. Leave in a cool place for at least 30 minutes, for the starch to begin to break down.

Meanwhile, well butter 4 ovenproof saucers. Put the fruit in an ovenproof dish and sprinkle with sugar, cover and put in the oven while it is heating up until the juices begin to run. Taste to see if sweet enough (be careful not to cook strawberries for more than a few seconds or they will go mushy). Take the fruit from the oven and leave on one side.

Whisk egg whites until very stiff, and fold into batter. Divide batter between 4 prepared saucers, and put in the top of a preheated oven at 230°C, 450°F, gas mark 8. Bake for about 15–20 minutes or until golden brown and coming away from the edges of the saucers. Remove from the oven when cooked, and slide on to a warmed serving dish. Sprinkle with caster sugar and fill each batter with fruit. Serve hot with whipped cream.

An Excellent Lemon Pudding

This lovely pudding is based on a very old recipe which was baked in a dish lined with puff pastry. By whisking egg whites and adding just before baking, the pudding will be very light. You may need to cover with greaseproof paper if the top is getting brown too quickly before the underneath has set. This pudding separates out during cooking into a tangy custard layer with a featherlight sponge topping. An orange or lime pudding can be made in the same way.

100g (3½oz) butter, softened
175g (6oz) caster sugar
Grated rind and juice of 4 lemons
4 eggs, separated
125ml (4fl oz) full-cream milk
50g (1¾oz) plain flour

Serves 4–6

Cream the butter and sugar together until white and fluffy, then beat in the lemon rind and juice. Beat the egg yolks into creamed mixture very gradually. When the mixture is very light, beat in the milk. Fold in the sieved flour.

Whisk the egg whites until they are firm and stand in peaks. Fold them gently into the lemon mixture, then pour into a buttered 20cm (8in) soufflé dish. Place the dish in a roasting tin and pour hot water into the tin until it comes halfway up the sides of the dish.

Bake in the centre of a preheated oven at 180°C, 350°F, gas mark 4, for about 45 minutes, until the top is golden brown and the pudding has risen.

Serve warm, or cold with cream.

Plum and Cinnamon Crumble

Crumbles can be varied, not just by using seasonal fruit but also by changing the crumble topping, adding porridge oats (as here), dessicated coconut, chopped nuts, different spices and so on. Classic combinations such as rhubarb and ginger, apple and cinnamon, gooseberry and elderflower, can always be relied on. This particular recipe was given to me by a good friend, who is chef at Cotehele, a medieval house belonging to the National Trust on the banks of the River Tamar, in Cornwall. He cooks the crumble in individual dishes under the grill.

600g (1 lb 5oz) English plums, stoned
50g (1¾oz) light brown sugar
¼ teaspoon ground cinnamon

FOR THE TOPPING
40g (1½oz) butter, cut in small pieces
55g (2oz) plain flour
½ teaspoon cinnamon
40g (1½oz) light brown sugar
60g (2oz) porridge oats

Serves 4

Poach the plums with the sugar and cinnamon and a very little water until just tender. Remove from the heat and tip into a buttered ovenproof baking dish. Rub the butter into the flour and cinnamon sieved together, into a mixing bowl until the mixture resembles breadcrumbs. Stir in the sugar and oats. Sprinkle evenly over the plums and bake in a preheated oven at 180°C, 350°F, gas mark 4 for about 25 minutes, or until golden brown. Remove from the oven and leave to cool a little. Eat warm and serve with Vanilla Custard Sauce (see below), Vanilla Ice Cream (see page 59) or clotted cream.

Vanilla Custard Sauce

6 large egg yolks
70g (2½oz) caster sugar
1 vanilla pod

300ml (½ pint) full-cream milk
300ml (½ pint) double cream

Beat the egg yolks and sugar together in a bowl until well blended. Split and scrape the seeds of the vanilla pod into a pan with the milk and cream and bring to the boil. Place the bowl over a pan of hot water and whisk the cream into the egg mixture. As the egg yolks warm, the cream will thicken to create a custard. Keep stirring until it coats the back of a spoon. Remove the bowl from the heat and serve warm or cold.

Rhubarb and Orange Betty

An original 19th-century Brown Betty was made with apples, breadcrumbs and suet and was a popular pudding with lower-paid countryfolk. Delicious Brown Betty can be made with other fruits, but the amount of sugar must be adjusted accordingly. Some of the most successful are rhubarb (as here), plums, gooseberries, damsons, blackcurrants, blackberries and cherries.

85g (3oz) butter
115g (4oz) fresh white breadcrumbs
450g (1lb) rhubarb
85-115g (3-4 oz) caster or soft brown sugar
Grated rind and juice of 1 orange

Serves 4–6

Melt the butter in a heavy frying pan, add the breadcrumbs and cook over moderate heat, stirring continuously to prevent burning, until the crumbs are light golden in colour.

Cut the rhubarb into 2.5cm (1in) lengths, then mix with the sugar, orange rind and juice. Butter a 1.2 litre (2 pint) ovenproof dish and fill with alternate layers of rhubarb and breadcrumbs, finishing with a layer of crumbs. Sprinkle with extra sugar and cover with foil. Bake in the centre of a preheated oven at 180°C, 350°F, gas mark 4 for 20 minutes, then remove the foil and continue cooking for a further 25–30 minutes, or until the top is brown and crisp and the rhubarb is soft.

Serve hot with Vanilla Custard Sauce (see page 29) or cream.

The Curate's Pudding

This recipe comes from the The Best of Eliza Acton, *first published in 1845. It's an excellent pudding best made with seasonal British fruits. I use thinly sliced brioche buns instead of 'penny rolls', but bread rolls or slices of bread work just as well.*

450g (1lb) young pink rhubarb
25g (1oz) butter
4 tablespoons caster sugar
2 brioche buns, thinly sliced

Serves 4

Cut the rhubarb into 2.5cm (1in) lengths. Melt the butter and brush the insides of a 1.2 litre (2 pint) soufflé dish or ovenproof dish with a little of it. Place half the rhubarb into the dish and sprinkle on about half the sugar. Cover the fruit with a layer of brioche slices.

Now lay on the remaining fruit and sprinkle on all but a teaspoon of the remaining sugar. Cover the rhubarb with slices of brioche, shaping to fit. Press down with your hand to flatten the pudding, then brush the top with the remaining butter. Sprinkle with remaining sugar and bake in a preheated oven at 180°C, 350°F, gas mark 4 for about 30 minutes, or until the fruit is tender and the top browned. Serve warm with cream.

Cherry Batter

This famous pudding from Kent has been eaten at cherry feasts and fairs since the 13th century, but probably the idea of combining cherries with batter came to the UK with the Normans. This dish is a reminder that Kent was one of the first counties to be colonized by the invaders. A very similar dish called Clafoutis is still made in some regions of France. Kent's famous juicy black morello cherries, said to be the best black cherries in the world, should be used to make this delicious pud, but drained tinned black cherries can be used out of season. Traditionally the pudding is served cold, but I prefer it warm.

50g (1¾oz) plain flour
Pinch of salt
50g (1¾oz) caster sugar
2 eggs
300ml (½ pint) single- or full-cream milk
1 tablespoon cherry brandy or a few drops of vanilla essence
25g (1oz) melted butter
450g (1lb) ripe black cherries, stoned
Icing sugar for dredging

Serves 6

Sieve flour and salt together into a bowl. Stir in the caster sugar. Beat eggs and blend gradually into flour mixture. Warm the cream or milk and add slowly to the flour mixture beating vigorously to make a smooth light batter. Stir in cherry brandy or vanilla essence and whisk in melted butter. Put aside to rest while you stone the cherries.

Generously butter a shallow 600ml (1 pint) ovenproof porcelain dish or a 20cm (8in) flan tin. Spread the prepared cherries over the bottom of the dish or tin and carefully pour over the batter. Dot with a few tiny pieces of butter and bake in the centre of a preheated oven at 200°C, 400°F, gas mark 6 for 20 minutes, then reduce temperature to 190°C, 375°F, gas mark 5 and cook for a further 20 minutes or until batter is well risen and golden, but still creamy inside. Serve warm, generously dredged with sieved icing sugar and with whipped cream or Vanilla Custard Sauce (see page 29). If you want to serve the pudding cold, remove from the dish or tin and serve with either pouring or whipped cream.

Right: Cherry Batter

Hollygog Pudding

This is a golden syrupy roly-poly which is baked in milk. It was first made in the Oxfordshire village of Kiddington, where it has been passed down among farming families.

225g (8oz) plain flour
Pinch of salt
115g (4oz) butter

About 3 tablespoons cold water
4 tablespoons golden syrup, warmed
About 300ml (½ pint) full-cream milk

Serves 4–6

Sieve flour and salt into a mixing bowl and rub fat into flour until mixture resembles breadcrumbs. Add water to form a stiff dough. Roll out into a rectangular strip, spread with syrup and roll up like a Swiss roll. Put in a well-buttered oval ovenproof dish and pour over enough milk to come halfway up the side of the pudding. Bake in a preheated oven at 200°C, 400°F, gas mark 6 for 40–45 minutes. Serve hot in slices with cream, Economical Custard Sauce (see below) or Vanilla Custard Sauce (see page 29).

Economical Custard Sauce

300ml (½ pint) full-cream milk
150ml (¼ pint) single cream
1 vanilla pod or strip or lemon peel
3 eggs

2 level tablespoons caster sugar
2 heaped tablespoons cornflour
4 tablespoons milk

Heat milk and cream in a saucepan (you can use all milk if you prefer) with vanilla pod or lemon peel. Bring to the boil. Remove from heat and leave to cool for a few seconds, removing vanilla pod or lemon peel. Beat eggs with sugar in a basin. Mix cornflour with 4 tablespoons milk until a smooth paste. Add this to the egg mixture and stir well. Pour hot milk slowly on to egg mixture, stirring continuously. Rinse out the saucepan, leaving a film of cold water in the bottom. Return custard to pan and stir with a wooden spoon over a low heat until thick (don't boil the custard or it will curdle). Strain into a jug and serve hot. If you don't want a skin to form on top of your custard, sprinkle the surface with caster sugar or cover closely with a piece of damp greaseproof paper or clingfilm.

Left: Hollygog Pudding

Creams, Flummeries, Fools, Snows and Syllabubs

England's elaborate and elegant cold sweets were famous throughout Europe in Tudor times. The sweet course at a great feast was then known as the 'banquet' and consisted of preserved fruits, creams, flummeries, jellies, fools and tarts. Some noblemen built banqueting houses in their grounds to serve the banquet privately to their guests after the main part of the meal had been eaten in the Great Hall. On prosperous farms these dishes were less elaborately served and decorated, but the same cold sweets, rich with cream, butter, eggs and fruit, were made for special occasions.

The ancestor of creams, fools and flummeries was the medieval meatless pottage known as 'frumenty', made from breadcrumbs, oats, rice, wheat or barley, stewed in almond milk and served on fasting days. Cream later replaced the milk and almonds were used for thickening. This dish was known as 'whitepot'. By the 17th century, the almonds were often omitted and the cream was thickened with eggs. Sometimes fresh or boiled cream was sweetened and mixed with fruit pulp to make fruit fools or creams.

In the 18th century, gooseberries and orange juice combined with eggs were made into fools, and recipes for almond and codlin or apple cream were very common. These fruit creams were served in the second course alongside flummeries and jellies. Iced creams and snows were also being made at this time.

The syllabub of Tudor and Stuart times was designed to be drunk and consisted of white wine, cider or fruit juice, sugar and nutmeg, to which cream or milk was whisked. The object was to produce a frothy head to the drink with a clear liquid below. The latter was drunk from the spout of a 'syllabub pot', while the creamy foam was eaten. In Georgian times the cream and wine were whisked together with lemon juice – these whipped-cream syllabubs remained a very popular dessert all through the 18th century and have become fashionable again in the last few years.

There are so many delicious recipes for these creamy puddings that it has been impossible to include even a reasonable number in this chapter, but I hope you will enjoy those I have mentioned and that they will inspire you to experiment with other fruits and flavourings yourselves.

Victorian Apple Snow

This dish of apples and whisked egg whites has ancient ancestors. Egg whites were first beaten in Elizabethan days and used to produce their 'dishful of snow', a spectacular centrepiece for the banquet course following a festive meal. They were beaten with thick cream, rose water and sugar until the froth rose and was gathered in a colander. This was built up over an apple and a bed of rosemary on a platter.

The same dish with the addition of whipped cream continued into the 18th century as Snow Cream or Blanched Cream. Another form with the addition of apple pulp came to be known as Apple Snow and other seasonal fruit pulps were also used. In Victorian times the cream was omitted and became the pudding that we know today.

1kg (2lb 4oz) Bramley apples
1 tablespoon lemon juice
3 tablespoons sweet cider or water
Grated rind of 1 lemon
About 85g (3oz) caster sugar
Pinch of ground cinnamon (optional)
3 egg whites
About 4 teaspoons golden muscovado sugar, to decorate
Edible fresh flowers, to decorate

Serves 6

Peel, core and thinly slice the apples. Put in a heavy saucepan with the lemon juice, cider or water, and lemon rind. Cover and cook over very low heat until quite soft and fluffy, stirring once or twice. Then remove the lid and continue cooking, stirring frequently, until the apples are reduced to a foam and most of the moisture has been driven off. Remove from the heat and stir in sugar to taste – remember that half the charm of this traditional dish is its light, fruity freshness, so it should be quite tart. Stir in cinnamon if using, then beat until smooth with a wooden spoon. Turn into a dish and leave to become cold.

Whisk egg whites until they stand in shiny peaks. Lightly fold in the cold apple purée and spoon into individual glasses. Refrigerate.

Immediately before serving, sprinkle with muscovado sugar and decorate with edible fresh flowers. Daisies look particularly lovely with this simple pudding. Eat with little dessert biscuits, homemade if possible.

Little Chocolate Pots

175g (6oz) good-quality plain chocolate
2 tablespoons water
15g (½oz) salted butter
3 eggs, separated

Serves 6

Break the chocolate into small pieces, then put in a basin with the water. Place over a pan of gently simmering water to melt the chocolate into a thick cream, stirring from time to time. Remove from the heat and stir in the butter. Beat in the egg yolks one at a time (they will be slightly cooked in the hot chocolate mixture). Leave to cool.

Whisk the egg whites until stiff, then briskly fold into the chocolate. When thoroughly mixed, pour into little custard pots or ramekins. Chill overnight.

Serve with homemade dessert biscuits.

Variations

Little Chocolate and Orange Pots
Stir in the grated rind of 1 large orange and 1 tablespoon orange liqueur into the melted chocolate with the butter.

Little Chocolate and Coffee Pots
Stir 1 tablespoon coffee essence or very strong espresso, into the melted chocolate with the butter.

Damson Snow

This also makes a super ice cream. Freeze in the normal way.

900g (2lb) damsons
175g (6oz) caster sugar
90ml (3fl oz) cold water
425ml (¾ pint) double cream
2 tablespoons brandy or Marsala (optional)
3 egg whites

Serves 6

Put washed and de-stalked damsons into a saucepan with sugar and water. Bring slowly to the boil and cook gently for 10–15 minutes or until fruit is tender. Rub through a sieve and leave damson pulp to get cold.

Lightly whip cream with brandy or Marsala if using until thick. Whisk egg whites until stiff and fold into cream mixture. Stir in damson pulp reserving 1 tablespoon for decoration. Pour into individual glasses and chill well. Just before serving, stir in reserved damson pulp to give a marbled effect, or just top with damson pulp. Serve with homemade dessert biscuits.

Variation

Edinburgh Fog

Omit the damsons. Whip the cream with 2 tablespoons sweet sherry or Madeira. Stir in 55g (2oz) ratafia biscuits and sweeten to taste with caster sugar. Chill well. Then sprinkle generously with toasted flaked almonds. Serve with fresh raspberries or strawberries.

Cranachan

A traditional Scottish pudding which started life as a hot drink similar to the Elizabethan version of syllabub and was later thickened with oatmeal. Fragrant heather honey, Scotch whisky and Scottish raspberries are traditional, but other fruits and alcohol can be used.

85g (3oz) coarse oatmeal
300ml (½ pint) double cream
50g (1¾oz) caster sugar
50ml (2fl oz) malt whisky
350g (12oz) fresh raspberries, reserving
   a few for decoration
Sprigs of fresh mint

Serves 4–6

Sprinkle the oatmeal on to a baking tray. Bake in a preheated oven at 200°C, 400°F, gas mark 6, until browned and crisp, moving the oatmeal around to prevent sticking and burning. Remove from the oven and cool.

Whip the cream with the sugar and whisky, until it stands in fairly soft peaks. Gently fold in the cooled toasted oatmeal. Spoon into individual glasses, layering the raspberries between spoonfuls of the mixture, as you go. Serve decorated with a few raspberries and a sprig of fresh mint.

Variation

Cranachan with Strawberries
Quarter 600g (1lb 5oz) strawberries and leave to soak in 25g (1oz) caster sugar and 50ml (2fl oz) raspberry liqueur for at least 10 minutes. Gently heat the oatmeal and 50g (1¾oz) soft brown sugar for 2–3 minutes, stirring continuously until the sugar has dissolved and the oatmeal is golden and caramelized. Remove from the heat and spread oatmeal on a plate to cool, breaking up any large clusters with a fork. Continue as before.

Whim-Wham

This Edwardian trifle used Naples biscuits, the foundation for many 18th- and 19th-century desserts, instead of sponge cakes, and syllabub instead of custard. It is very rich, so serve small portions.

300ml (½ pint) double cream
55g (2oz) caster sugar
2 tablespoons white wine
Grated rind of 1 lemon
12 sponge finger or boudoir biscuits
225g (8oz) redcurrant, quince or apple jelly
25g (1oz) chopped candied orange peel

Serves 6

Put cream, sugar, wine and lemon rind into a large bowl and whisk until thick. Break biscuits into several pieces and spoon layers of syllabub, biscuits and jelly alternately in an attractive glass bowl, ending with a layer of syllabub. Sprinkle with chopped candied orange peel and chill overnight.

Right: Whim-Wam
Next page: Cranachan

Lemon Posset

A posset was an Elizabethan drink made of milk curdled with sack (sack is the old name of a Spanish wine rather like sherry) or claret, beer, ale and orange or lemon juice – rather like a syllabub. Breadcrumbs were added to thicken the posset so that it could be eaten rather than drunk. Later, these were omitted and beaten egg whites were used instead to make it lighter and not so rich.

600ml (1 pint) double or whipping cream
Grated rind of 1½ lemons
150ml (¼ pint) dry white wine
4 tablespoons lemon juice
About 115g (4oz) caster sugar
3 large egg whites
2 tablespoons caster sugar
Extra lemon zest for decorating

Serves 6

Beat cream and lemon rind in a mixing bowl until thick. Beat in the wine until thick again. Add the lemon juice very gradually, beating all the time. Add sugar to taste and beat until stiff. Whisk egg whites until stiff and standing in peaks, then whisk in the 2 tablespoons sugar until smooth and glossy. Fold the egg whites into the cream mixture, then pile into a glass of china bowl. Serve chilled and decorated with lemon zest. Accompany with homemade dessert biscuits.

Variation

Orange Posset
Substitute grated rind of 1 orange for 1 lemon and 2 tablespoons orange juice for 2 tablespoons of the lemon juice. Decorate with orange zest.

Left: Lemon Posset
Previous page: Rhubarb and Orange Fool

Rhubarb and Orange Fool

Rhubarb was one of the last garden fruits to be cultivated for eating in Britain. It had been grown in China for its root, a powerful purgative, which was exported to Europe. In Tudor times the plants themselves were introduced into English herb gardens and medicinal rhubarb became a garden crop. The rhubarb we know now first arrived in the 17th century when John Parkinson received seeds from Italy which he planted in his garden. Its cultivation spread rapidly throughout Britain and it has remained one of the most popular garden fruits.

An old-fashioned rhubarb or spring fool is the perfect way to round off a spring dinner party, especially if the meal has been rather rich. Young forced rhubarb makes the best fool, because of its beautiful pink colour when cooked.

900g (2lb) rhubarb
Grated rind of 1 orange
½ teaspoon ground ginger
5cm (2in) stick cinnamon
25g (1oz) unsalted butter
About 175g (6oz) caster sugar
600ml (1 pint) double or whipping cream
2 tablespoons orange liqueur (optional)
Primroses or other spring flowers to decorate

Serves 8–10

Cut the rhubarb into short lengths. Put in a large saucepan with orange rind, ginger, cinnamon stick, butter and sugar. Cook over a gentle heat for about five minutes until the rhubarb is softened, thick and pulpy. Remove cinnamon stick and cool completely.

Whip the cream with the liqueur if using until thick enough to hold its shape. Fold in cold rhubarb pulp very lightly to give a marbled effect. Taste, and add more sugar if necessary. Spoon fool into a deep glass bowl or individual glasses, and chill well before serving. Decorate with primroses, or other simple edible spring flowers.

London Syllabub

Syllabub is one of the oldest known British dishes. London Syllabub is one example of a typical Georgian syllabub of the 'everlasting' type, which meant that it didn't separate into a honey-combed curd on the top with an alcoholic drink underneath.

Allow the lemon or orange rind and rosemary to infuse in the fruit juice and the alcohol overnight if possible.

Finely pared rind of 1 lemon or 2 oranges
Juice of 1 lemon or orange
Sprig of fresh rosemary, bruised
150ml (¼ pint) white wine, dry sherry or Madeira
2 tablespoons brandy
85g (3oz) caster sugar or honey
300ml (½ pint) double cream
Sprigs of fresh rosemary for decorating

Serves 4–6

Put lemon or orange rind and juice and rosemary in a bowl with the wine and brandy and leave overnight. Next day, strain wine and orange or lemon mixture into a saucepan. Add sugar or honey and heat gently until sugar has dissolved. Pour into a large deep bowl and leave to cool. Gradually stir in the cream, beating until it 'ribbons' and stands in soft peaks (don't use an electric blender or the cream may become grainy). Pour into individual glasses, or custard cups, and chill. Serve decorated with sprigs of rosemary. Also very good with Apple Fritters (see page 64).

Variations

Lavender Syllabub
Flavour with 2 sprigs of lavender, bruised well, instead of the rosemary. Serve decorated with lavender flowers. Many other herbs and flowers can be used to flavour syllabub. Lemon geranium leaves are also very successful. Use 8 bruised leaves to 300ml (½ pint) cream.

Spiced Syllabub
Infuse the rind of 1 orange, 1 lemon, 1 stick of cinnamon and 8 cloves in 200ml (7fl oz) decent red wine overnight, then continue as before. Serve decorated with orange zest.

Elderflower Trifle

Elderflowers were used widely in the past to flavour jellies, creams, flummeries, fools and trifles. Pick on a dry day. This trifle has a base of Amaretti or ratafia biscuits, with a syllabub topping. It looks prettiest in individual stemmed glasses.

FOR THE SYLLABUB
Grated rind and juice of 1 large lemon
1 large elderflower head in full bloom
125ml (4fl oz) white wine
85g (3oz) caster sugar
Pinch of freshly grated nutmeg
300ml (½ pint) double cream
Sprigs of elderflower to decorate

FOR THE BASE
8 Amaretti biscuits
2 tablespoons homemade or good-quality elderflower cordial
2 tablespoons sweet sherry
2 tablespoons cold water

Serves 4

Begin by making the liquid base for the syllabub. Mix together the lemon rind, juice and flowers snipped from the elderflower head. Set aside to steep for at least 1 hour.

Meanwhile, put the biscuits, broken, into 4 glasses. Mix the cordial, sherry and water together and pour equal amounts into each glass.

Strain the steeped syllabub liquid into a large bowl. Stir in the sugar and the nutmeg, then pour in the cream. Whisk together until the cream thickens, then spoon into the glasses.

Serve chilled and decorated with a few tiny sprigs of elderflower, either fresh or crystallized. Elderflower can be crystallized by dipping it into beaten egg white, then into sugar and leaving it on a wire rack to dry.

Gooseberry and Elderflower Fool

'Soft, pale, creamy, untroubled, the English fruit fool is the most frail and insubstantial of English summer dishes', wrote Elizabeth David. The fruit fool, probably named after the French verb fouler, *meaning 'to crush', is one of the few quintessentially English puddings that should not be tampered with – for me, the perfect fool is just cream, fruit (flavoured or plain) and sugar.*

Gooseberry fool has been very popular for centuries, but was particularly loved by the Victorians, who added egg-thickened custard. In this recipe I have gone back to basics, but flavoured the gooseberries with elderflowers, which are flowering at the same time. If you want to use frozen gooseberries out of season, elderflower cordial can be used instead, with less sugar. The fool mixture can be frozen as an ice cream.

450g (1lb) green gooseberries
3 or 4 large elderflower heads in full bloom
1 tablespoon water
85–115g (3–4oz) caster sugar
300ml (½ pint) double cream

Serves 4–6

Wash and top and tail gooseberries. Put in a heavy saucepan with the elderflower heads tied together with cotton thread, the water and the sugar. Cook gently until the fruit is soft, then set aside to cool. Once cool, lift out the elderflower stalks – don't worry about leaving the flowers behind, they will add to the flavour.

Mash the gooseberries with a fork and taste for sweetness (if you prefer a smoother purée, rub the gooseberries through a plastic sieve). Leave to get completely cold.

Whip double cream until thick and just beginning to hold its shape. Fold into gooseberry purée to give a swirled, marbled effect, then pile into a serving bowl or individual glasses. Decorate with small sprigs of elderflower, if in season. Serve with homemade biscuits.

Variations

Any fruits can be used to make fools, but for me, the most successful are berries, currants, apricots, the plum family and of course, rhubarb.

Lemon Solid

This pudding's ancestor was the posset, but instead of being thickened with breadcrumbs, eggs and almond-flavoured biscuit crumbs, or ground almonds were used. Lemon Solid is found in varying forms, in many old cookery books and is one of the glories of British cooking, despite its rather uninspiring name.

600ml (1 pint) thick double cream
Grated rind and juice of 2 lemons
115g (4oz) caster sugar
3–4 macaroons, homemade if possible

Serves 6–8

Put cream, lemon rind and sugar in a saucepan. Stir over gentle heat for about 10 minutes until sugar has completely dissolved, bringing just to the boil. Cool, stirring from time to time and when almost cold add strained lemon juice. Crumble macaroons and put in the bottom of an attractive glass bowl. Pour cold cream mixture over macaroons. Chill overnight in the refrigerator.

Serve chilled and decorated with lemon zest.

Gooseberry Tansy

This very old pudding was so-called from the use of the herb tansy. It was chopped up with the fruit, but is seldom used in cookery today as it has rather a bitter flavour. Apples, rhubarb or plums can be used instead of gooseberries.

450g (1lb) green gooseberries
115g (4oz) unsalted butter
2 egg yolks
150ml (¼ pint) double cream
About 2 tablespoons caster sugar
Juice of ½ lemon

Serves 4

Simmer gooseberries in the butter until cooked – about 15 minutes. Remove from heat and cool a little. Stir in beaten egg yolks and lightly whipped cream. Sweeten with sugar to taste. Bring to the boil very gently and when thick, turn into a china serving bowl. Sprinkle with caster sugar and lemon juice. Serve cold.

Fine Orange Flummery

Flummery, a lovely pale slippery pudding related to syllabub and custard, is a delicious pure white jelly. In medieval times, cereals such as rice, oats or sago were cooked long and slowly with milk and flavourings. This was really the beginning of the flummery. In Tudor and Stuart times it became a much richer dish of cream flavoured with spices, orange flower water, rose water, almonds or wine, set with calves' feet or isinglass. It was often coloured and eaten in the second course with cream or wine poured over. For special occasions, it was made in the most elaborate moulds for 'set-piece dishes', such as flummery fish in a pond of jelly, or flummery eggs in a hen's nest of shredded lemon peel set in jelly.

Flummery is now easily set with gelatine and should be made in the most attractive mould you can find. It is still possible to pick up fairly cheaply elaborate Victorian china and glass jelly moulds in antique and junk shops. If possible, this dish should be made the day before you want to serve it.

600ml (1 pint) double cream
50g (1¾oz) caster sugar
Grated rind and juice of 2 oranges

1 tablespoon orange flower water
3 tablespoons warm water
15g (½oz) gelatine

Serves 6

Put cream, sugar, orange rind and juice and orange flower water in a heavy saucepan and heat very gently until sugar is completely dissolved and cream is just coming to the boil. Leave on one side to cool. Put warm water into a cup and sprinkle over gelatine. Stand the cup in a pan of water and heat gently, stirring, until the gelatine has dissolved. Pour through a warmed sieve into cream mixture. Stir well. Pour into a wetted mould and leave to cool. Refrigerate overnight.

To turn out, dip mould quickly in hot water. Serve chilled with a bowl of soft fruit and whipped cream.

Variations

Fine Orange and Madeira Flummery
Replace orange flower water with Madeira or sweet sherry.

Almond Flummery
Omit orange flower water, orange rind and juice. Replace with 115g (4oz) ground almonds and 4–5 drops almond essence.

Boodles Orange Fool

A speciality at Boodles Club in St James' Street, London, which was founded in 1762. It sounds simple, but is very delicious. The idea of combining sponge with fruit fool dates back to the 18th-century version with ratafias.

4 sponge cakes
Grated rind and juice of 1 lemon
Grated rind and juice of 2 oranges
55–85g (2–3oz) caster sugar
600ml (1 pint) double cream
Crystallized orange slices
Crystallized angelica

Serves 4–6

Cut sponge cakes into 1cm (½ in) strips and line the base of a glass serving dish, or individual glass dishes. Mix rind and juice of fruit with sugar and stir until dissolved. Whip half the cream until thick but not stiff, and beat juice into cream slowly. Taste for sweetness. Spoon over sponge cakes and chill thoroughly for 2–3 hours, until juice has soaked into sponge and cream has set. Whip remaining cream until stiff, and pipe on top of pudding to decorate. Decorate with crystallized orange slices and angelica.

Iced Creams

Iced Cream became popular in Britain in the 18th century with the development of ice houses on country estates. Large quantities of ice were stored in specially built brick or stone-lined pits to last the whole year, or more, if possible. When the winter was cold enough, this ice was taken from local ponds, lakes and rivers, otherwise it was brought from Scotland and Norway. Later, with better sea transport, ice came back in the holds of ships, as ballast, from North America.

The earliest ice creams were literally iced fruit creams of frozen fruit fools and were prepared in tall pewter pots with close-fitting lids, buried in pails filled with ice and salt. The first mechanical ice cream maker was invented in the middle of the 19th century and made life a lot easier.

You can still make delicious ice cream by freezing fruit purée and cream, but by adding beaten eggs a lighter ice is produced which also softens more quickly for serving. It is great fun experimenting with ice creams and the possible variations, both simple and elaborate, seem endless. My favourite basic recipe was my mother-in-law's. She was a wonderful cook and a very special friend.

Don't worry if you haven't an ice cream maker – use a lidded plastic container instead and stir from time to time as the mixture freezes.

Blackcurrant Ice Cream

This is an ice cream made using the custard method. Fresh or frozen berries, or homemade jam, sharpened with a squeeze of lemon – in which case omit the sugar – are successful. Any fruits can be used to make ice cream, but my favourites are damson, raspberry, a combination of rhubarb and redcurrant and blackberry as well as blackcurrant.

300ml (½ pint) double cream
300ml (½ pint) full-cream milk
4 eggs, separated
8 tablespoons caster sugar
450g (1lb) blackcurrants

Serves 6–8

Whisk the cream, milk, egg yolks and sugar together in a basin. Set over a pan of simmering water and continue whisking until the custard thickens enough to coat the spoon. Leave to cool.

Pick over the blackcurrants if using fresh fruit and remove any stalks. Liquidize the fruit to a thick purée and stir into the cooled custard.

Freeze the mixture until the edges are solid, but the middle is still soft – an hour or two. Beat the half-frozen mixture and fold in the egg whites, stiffly whisked. Freeze again until solid. Place in the refrigerator for 30 minutes before serving with thick cream.

Brown Bread Ice Cream

Introduced later in the 18th century than the fruit ice creams, brown bread ice cream was not popular until late Victorian and Edwardian days, when it was served as a country weekend treat. The breadcrumbs can be fried, baked or grilled with the sugar.

85g (3oz) brown breadcrumbs
85g (3oz) soft dark brown sugar
3 large eggs, separated
½ tablespoon rum
300ml (½ pint) double cream
85g (3oz) icing sugar, sifted

Serves 4–6

Preheat the oven to 200°C, 400°F, gas mark 6. Grease a baking sheet with butter. In a bowl, mix together the breadcrumbs and sugar, then spread over the baking sheet. Bake for about 15 minutes until dark and caramelized, stirring now and again. Cool, then break up the crumbs with a fork.

Whisk the egg whites until stiff. Mix the egg yolks with the rum, then fold into the whites. Whisk the cream and icing sugar until floppy, then fold into the egg mixture, with the breadcrumbs. Pour into a shallow plastic lidded container and freeze in the normal way, beating frequently as it freezes. Remove from the freezer to the refrigerator at least 30 minutes before serving with a hot or cold fruit sauce, such as damson, plum, blackcurrant or blackberry or Easy Chocolate Sauce (see page 56).

Elderflower Ice Cream

This creamy ice cream is very simple to make, particularly if you use a commercial elderflower cordial rather than making your own.

2 large egg whites
1 tablespoon caster sugar
300ml (½ pint) double cream

90ml (3fl oz) good-quality elderflower cordial
Sprigs of elderflower, to decorate

Serves 4–6

Whisk the egg whites until stiff and beat in the sugar. Whip the cream until it stands in soft peaks, then beat in the elderflower cordial.

Fold the egg whites into the cream and turn the mixture into a lidded plastic container. Freeze for 4–5 hours until firm. Allow to soften in the refrigerator for 30 minutes before serving, scooped in stemmed glasses and decorated with elderflower, if in season.

Stem Ginger Ice Cream

This is a delicious ice cream and ideal for serving at Christmas lunch as an alternative to Christmas pud or as a refreshing alternative to Brandy Butter. It is very good served with meringues flavoured with ground ginger.

4 eggs, separated
110g (4oz) caster sugar
1 teaspoon ground ginger
2 tablespoons brandy

425ml (¾ pint) double or whipping cream
6 large pieces stem ginger in syrup, chopped

Serves 6–8

Beat egg yolks with the sugar, ground ginger and brandy. Whip cream until it stands in soft peaks and add to the egg mixture. Whisk egg whites until stiff and fold into the mixture. Pour into a lidded container and freeze for about 1 hour. Add 4 of the pieces of chopped stem ginger and stir evenly into semi-set ice cream. Return to freezer until completely set.

Scoop into glasses, sprinkle with remaining chopped ginger and pour over a little of the stem ginger syrup. Top with Easy Chocolate, Ginger or Butterscotch Sauce (see pages 56, 140 and 154).

Honey and Brandy Ice Cream

4 large eggs, separated
115g (4oz) caster sugar
4 tablespoons clear honey, warmed
425ml (¾ pint) double cream
6 tablespoons brandy or cider brandy

Serves 6–8

Beat the egg yolks and sugar until pale in colour. Add the warmed honey a little at a time, beating continuously, until pale and fluffy, then put to one side. Whisk the cream with the brandy until it forms soft peaks. Whisk egg whites in a separate bowl, until stiff. Pour the egg mixture into a large bowl, then fold in a quarter of the cream, followed by a quarter of the egg white. Repeat until all the cream and egg whites have been incorporated into the yolk mixture. Pour into a lidded plastic container and freeze in the usual way.

This recipe makes a softer ice cream than usual because of the alcohol content, so it can be served straight from the freezer.

Scoop into bowls or glasses and serve with Butterscotch or Coffee Sauce (see pages 154 and 155), or with a little poached seasonal fruit, such as rhubarb, gooseberries or plums.

Lemon Mint Ice Cream

4 large eggs, separated
115g (4oz) caster sugar
300ml (½ pint) double cream
Grated rind and juice of 2 large lemons
4 sprigs of strongly flavoured fresh mint

Serves 4–6

Whisk the egg whites until stiff, then whisk in the sugar a little at a time, until the mixture is light and stands in peaks. Beat the egg yolks until pale, then fold into the egg white until thoroughly mixed. Whip the cream with the lemon rind and juice and add to the egg mixture. Chop the mint finely and fold into the mixture, then turn into a lidded plastic container and freeze as usual.

Chestnut Ice Cream

*Years ago, chestnuts were grown and used in cooking much more than they are today.
You will find this ice cream very delicate and unusual in flavour. Use fresh or tinned
unsweetened chestnut purée. You can melt 85g (3oz) good-quality plain chocolate and
add to the ice cream after the first stage of freezing, if preferred.*

4 eggs, separated
115g (4oz) caster or soft brown sugar
2–3 drops vanilla essence
225g (8oz) unsweetened chestnut
  purée

450ml (16fl oz) double or
  whipping cream
Marrons glacés to decorate
  (optional)

Serves 6–8

Beat egg yolks with sugar and vanilla essence. Stir in chestnut purée. Whip cream until it stands in soft
peaks and add to chestnut mixture. Whisk egg whites until stiff and fold gently into mixture. Pour into
a lidded container and freeze for about 1½ hours until mushy.

Remove ice cream from freezer and stir gently. Replace in freezer and leave to freeze completely.
Take ice cream out of freezer 30 minutes before you want to serve it, and leave in refrigerator to
soften and improve in flavour. Scoop into stemmed glasses and top with Easy Chocolate Sauce (see
below) and decorate with marrons glacés, if desired. Particularly good at Christmas.

Easy Chocolate Sauce

250g (9oz) good-quality plain chocolate
2 tablespoons strong black coffee, such
  as espresso

300ml (½ pint) whipping cream
Walnut-sized knob of butter

Break the chocolate into small pieces and put into a heavy saucepan with the coffee and the cream.
Heat slowly, stirring from time to time, until the chocolate has melted. Once the chocolate is
softened, stir until smooth, then stir in the butter. Pour into a warm jug and serve. Suitable for
pouring over poached pears, ice cream, chocolate pudding and meringues.

Right: Chestnut Ice Cream with Easy Chocolate Sauce
Next page: Nesselrode Pudding

Marmalade Ripple Ice Cream

Any marmalade may be used in this recipe depending on your personal taste, but top-quality thick-cut Seville is too strong except for the most dedicated marmalade lovers.

4 large eggs, separated
1 tablespoon lemon juice
115g (4oz) caster sugar

425ml (¾ pint) double or
   whipping cream
4–8 tablespoons marmalade (to taste)
1 tablespoon orange liqueur

Serves 6–8

Beat egg yolks with the lemon juice and caster sugar, until pale and frothy. Whip the cream until it stands in soft peaks and add to the egg mixture. Whisk the egg whites until soft and fold gently into the mixture. Pour into a lidded plastic container and freeze. When the mixture is almost frozen, mix together the marmalade and orange liqueur, then fold into the ice cream to create a ripple effect.

Ratafia Ice Cream

115g (4oz) ratafia biscuits
150ml (¼ pint) sweet sherry
4 eggs, separated
85g (3oz) caster sugar

425ml (¾ pint) double or
   whipping cream
25g (1oz) chopped toasted
   almonds

Serves 6–8

Crush ratafia biscuits and soak in sherry for 20 minutes. Beat egg yolks and sugar until thick and pale yellow in colour. Whip cream until it stands in peaks and add to egg mixture. Fold in soaked ratafia biscuits. Whisk egg whites until stiff and fold into mixture. Freeze in a lidded container for about 1 hour and then beat mixture and add chopped toasted almonds. Replace in the freezer and leave to set completely.

    About 30 minutes before serving, move from freezer into refrigerator and leave to soften. Serve topped with Eliza Acton's Madeira Sauce (see page 134) or with seasonal soft fruit and cream.

Left: Ratafia Ice Cream
Previous page: Marmalade Ripple Ice Cream

Nesselrode Pudding

This pudding was invented in the 19th century by Monsieur Mony, chef to the famous Count Nesselrode after whom it was named. It is reputed to be the most famous of the iced puddings, and was always produced at Christmas. This particular recipe is based on one I found in an unusual recipe book called The Ice Book*, written in 1844 by Thomas Masters. If frozen in a fancy mould it would make a terrific alternative Christmas pudding.*

FOR THE VANILLA SYRUP
150ml (¼ pint) water
50g (1¾oz) granulated sugar
1 vanilla pod, split in half lengthways

FOR THE ICE CREAM
25g (1oz) candied peel, chopped
25g (1oz) raisins
25g (1oz) glacé cherries, quartered

25g (1oz) currants
2 egg yolks
50g (1¾oz) caster sugar
300ml (½ pint) single cream
225g (8oz) fresh or tinned
   unsweetened chestnut purée
1 tablespoon Maraschino liqueur
150ml (¼ pint) double or
   whipping cream

Serves 6

To make the vanilla syrup, bring water, sugar and vanilla pod slowly to the bowl, stirring to dissolve the sugar. Boil rapidly for 5 minutes. Remove from heat and cool. When completely cold, remove the vanilla pod. (This can be washed and used again, so it is not as expensive as it might seem.)

Poach candied peel, raisins, cherries and currants in the prepared vanilla syrup for a few minutes. Drain, reserving syrup, and leave to cool.

Make a custard by beating egg yolks with the sugar until thick and pale yellow in colour. Heat the single cream to simmering point in a heavy-based saucepan, and stir into egg mixture. Strain back into the saucepan and stir continuously over gentle heat until the mixture thickens enough to coat the back of a spoon. Do not allow to boil. Pour into a large mixing bowl and leave to cool.

Mix the chestnut purée with reserved vanilla syrup and add to cooled custard with Maraschino. Stir well and pour into a lidded container. Freeze for 1 hour and then remove. Whip the cream until it stands in soft peaks and add to semi-set ice cream together with prepared raisins and currants. Freeze again until firm.

Serve topped with vanilla-flavoured cream and decorate with crystallized violets and angelica. This pudding looks very attractive frozen in a mould, turned out and then decorated with piped cream and grated chocolate or glacé cherries, crystallized violets or apricots – make it as elaborate and decorative as you wish.

Vanilla Ice Cream

If you want a vanilla ice cream with real flavour, this recipe is for you, but leave the vanilla pod whole if you prefer a more neutral-base ice cream.

1 vanilla pod
300ml (½ pint) full-cream milk
3 large egg yolks
About 115g (4oz) caster sugar
300ml (½ pint) double cream

Serves 6

Split the vanilla pod lengthways, then using a small knife strip out the seeds on to a white plate, so that you don't lose any. Put the seeds on one side for later.

Put the milk and vanilla pod (without the seeds) into a saucepan. Bring slowly to the boil, stirring occasionally. Draw off the heat, cover and leave for 20 minutes to infuse.

Whisk the egg yolks in a bowl with the sugar and vanilla seeds, then whisk in the vanilla-infused milk including the pod. Set the bowl over a pan of gently simmering water and cook, stirring continuously, until the custard thickens and covers the back of a wooden spoon. Taste and add more sugar if you wish. Leave to cool, then strain.

Whip the cream lightly and fold into the custard, then pour into a lidded plastic container and freeze as usual.

Half an hour before serving, transfer to the refrigerator to soften, before serving – divine with Rich Chocolate Pudding (see page 136).

Variation

Vanilla and Walnut

The addition of toasted walnuts makes a stunning ice cream. Spread 85g (3oz) chopped walnuts on to a baking tray and toast in a preheated oven at 200°C, 400°F, gas mark 6 for 4–7 minutes, shaking them once or twice. Tip into a metal sieve and shake to dislodge flakes of papery skin which should be discarded. Leave to cool. When your ice cream is semi-frozen, fold in the toasted walnuts. Return to the freezer to set solid.

Fried Puddings

Fried puddings were some of the earliest puddings to be made as the method was so simple and they could be cooked directly over the fire. Eggs were mixed with flour to make pancakes, although they were not considered important enough to be listed in recipe books. Some were made from egg whites only and these were much admired and served as fritters, sprinkled with sugar. These appeared regularly on medieval menus as part of the last course – apple, parsnip and carrot fritters were the most popular.

In Tudor and Stuart times, milk or water and spices were added to pancake batter, and the Georgians used cream as well as brandy to enrich the batter. Fritters continued to be popular, although again the batter was further enriched.

Heavy suet pudding mixtures were also fried as an alternative to boiling. The method was much faster and easier. The mixture was formed into small cakes or balls and fried or stewed in butter.

The important thing to remember when cooking fried puddings is that the fat or butter must be at the right temperature, particularly when deep frying. Also, most must be prepared at the last minute, although if you have a freezer they can be frozen once cooked and reheated when ready to serve.

Poor Knights of Windsor

A traditional pudding from Berkshire – where the alleged poverty of medieval knights was jokingly commemorated – consisting of bread, soaked in sherry or wine, eggs and cream, and fried. The recipe probably originated from France and was called Pain Perdu *or 'Lost Bread'. It is an excellent way of using up leftover bread or rolls. Also known in Georgian times as Spanish Fritters.*

6 thick slices of white bread
2 eggs
2 teaspoons caster sugar
150ml (¼ pint) single cream or milk
Pinch of ground cinnamon
Grated rind of ½ lemon
2 tablespoons Madeira or sweet sherry
Butter and oil for frying
Extra caster sugar and cinnamon, for sprinkling
Orange or lemon wedges, for serving

Serves 6

Remove crusts from bread and cut each slice into 3 fingers. Beat eggs and sugar together in a basin. Heat cream or milk until it just reaches boiling point. Cool a little before pouring on to egg mixture, beating continuously. Stir in cinnamon, lemon rind and Madeira or sherry.

Melt a little butter and oil in a heavy frying pan. Dip each finger or piece of bread into the custard mixture and fry until golden brown and crisp. Drain on crumpled kitchen paper and keep warm until all the bread has been fried. Sprinkle with caster sugar and ground cinnamon. Serve with orange or lemon wedges.

Variation

Eggy Bread with Maple Fried Apples

Melt 15g (½oz) butter in a frying pan and add 2 crisp dessert apples, unpeeled, cored and thickly sliced, 1 tablespoon pure maple syrup and a generous pinch of ground cinnamon. Cook over medium heat for about 10 minutes until the apples are just tender. Cook the pudding as before, then serve the fingers of fried bread topped with the apples and pan juices. Serve with thick cream if you wish.

Elderflower Fritters

Make the batter just before you cook the fritters and eat piping hot. Pick the flowers on a sunny morning.

8 elderflower heads in perfect condition, each with 1cm (½in) of stalk
115g (4oz) self-raising flour
Fizzy water to mix
Sunflower oil for frying
Icing sugar, for dusting
Thick cream, for serving

Serves 4

Shake each elderflower head to remove any insects. Sieve the flour into a bowl and mix in enough water, until you have a batter the texture of single cream. Heat about 2.5cm (1in) depth of sunflower oil in a pan until it sizzles when a drop of water is dropped in at arm's length. Working quickly, hold the stalk of a flower head and dip it into the batter. Lower it into the hot oil and fry until light golden. Remove from the pan and drain on kitchen paper. Serve immediately dusted with icing sugar and with thick cream.

Apple Fritters

Egg-batter fritters have been popular since medieval days. The most common fritters in Britain were made with apples, although later oranges, pineapple, bananas and pieces of pumpkin became popular.

115g (4oz) plain flour

Pinch of salt

½ teaspoon ground cinnamon

150ml (¼ pint) tepid water

2 tablespoons orange liqueur

1 tablespoon vegetable oil

4 medium cooking or crisp
   dessert apples

Grated rind and juice of ½ lemon

50g (1¾oz) icing sugar

25g (1oz) caster sugar

6 tablespoons apricot jam or thick
   orange marmalade

2 tablespoons water

Fat for deep frying (lard or oil)

2 egg whites

Caster sugar for dredging

Orange or lemon segments, for serving

Serves 6

Sieve flour, salt and cinnamon together into a basin. Make a well in the centre. Gradually blend in tepid water and 1 tablespoon liqueur, followed by oil. Beat vigorously with a rotary hand or electric whisk to make a smooth, glossy batter. Cover and leave to stand in a cool place for at least 30 minutes, to allow starch grains in the flour to absorb water and swell.

Peel, core and slice apples in 6mm (¼in) thick slices. Mix together lemon rind and juice, 1 tablespoon liqueur and sieved icing sugar. Add apple slices and coat evenly. In a heavy saucepan dissolve caster sugar and jam over a low heat. Dilute with water to make a syrup of coating consistency. Simmer syrup for 1 minute and keep warm. Coat each soaked apple ring in this syrup, allowing excess to drain off. Leave apple rings on one side to dry out a little.

When ready to cook fritters, heat fat for deep frying to 190°C, 375°F, gas mark 5. When a blue vapour rises from the fat, it is hot enough. Test by dropping in a little batter, which will rise if the fat is the correct temperature; if not, the batter will sink. Make sure your fat is absolutely clean and at least 7.5cm (3in) deep. Whisk egg whites until very stiff and fold into prepared batter. Using cooking tongs or a long skewer, dip apple rings, one at a time, into batter, allowing excess to drain off. Lower carefully into hot fat and deep-fry until crisp and puffed, turning them over once or twice. Avoid frying too many at once, because this cools the fat and does not allow room for fritters to expand properly. When cooked, remove from fat and drain on crumpled kitchen paper. Serve immediately dredged with caster sugar and thick cream or with Orange and Lemon Sauce (see page 156).

Right: Apple Fritters

A Quire of Paper

Much admired by 17th- and 18th-century cooks, a quire of paper consisted of a pile of wafer-thin pancakes. The batter, rich with eggs and cream, was run as thinly as possible over the bottom of a heavy pan and cooked on one side only. The completed pancakes were dredged with caster sugar and laid evenly one upon another until the pile contained twenty. A wine sauce and melted butter were served with the pancakes, which were cut into wedges like a cake.

This recipe will make a pile of about ten thin pancakes, but if you use a smaller 18cm (7in) pan you can make more. The pancakes can be spread individually with jam, jelly or fruit purée and cream.

115g (4oz) plain flour
Pinch of salt
25g (1oz) caster sugar
2 eggs
2 egg yolks
Unsalted butter for frying
300ml (½ pint) single cream or half cream and milk
2 tablespoons medium sherry or Madeira
Caster sugar, for sprinkling

Serves 6

Sieve flour and salt together into a basin. Stir in the sugar. Make a well in the centre of the flour. Put eggs and egg yolks into the well and gradually mix eggs and flour together. Add cream (or cream and milk) gradually, beating well until a smooth batter is formed. Stir in the sherry or Madeira to make a thin cream.

Heat a heavy-based pancake or omelet pan, brush with melted butter and add 1 tablespoon of batter. Twist the pan until the bottom is evenly coated with batter and cook until pancake is golden brown on the bottom. Remove from pan or turn over and cook the other side. Keep warm in a clean tea towel. Make a stack of pancakes, filling them with jam and whipped cream or whatever you choose. Sprinkle liberally with caster sugar.

Serve hot, cut in wedges with Eliza Acton's Madeira Sauce (see page 134).

Left: A Quire of Paper

New College Puddings

Traditionally served at New College, Oxford, in the 19th century, they first appeared in a recipe book by Dr William Kitchiner published in 1831. They were basically suet puddings which were fried instead of boiled, reducing the cooking time considerably. Oxford Dumplings were very similar.

115g (4oz) suet
115g (4oz) fresh white breadcrumbs
50g (1¾oz) caster or soft brown sugar
15g (½oz) baking powder
Pinch of salt
½ teaspoon grated nutmeg
Grated rind of 1 orange
115g (4oz) currants
25g (1oz) candied peel
3 eggs, separated
2 tablespoons brandy (optional)
Butter, for frying

Serves 6

Mix suet, breadcrumbs, sugar, baking powder, salt and nutmeg with orange rind, currants and candied peel, stirring thoroughly. Beat egg yolks and mix with brandy, if using. Stir into pudding mixture. Whisk egg whites and gently fold into pudding which should be a soft dropping consistency. Melt some butter in a heavy frying pan and fry tablespoonfuls of pudding mixture in hot butter, flattening the mixture as you cook it (like a fish cake). Turn once, frying each side for about 6 minutes until brown. Serve hot, sprinkled with sugar, and with Vanilla Custard Sauce (see page 29).

Traditional Lemon Pancakes

Although probably not of British origin, pancakes have been established here for so many centuries that they may be considered a national institution. When Lent was strictly observed, eggs and fatty foods were forbidden for forty days and so pancake-making became associated with Shrove Tuesday in the UK, to use up any remaining eggs, butter and milk before the fasting.

115g (4oz) plain flour
Pinch of salt
Grated rind of 1 lemon
1 egg
300ml (½ pint) milk

15g (½oz) melted butter
Butter, for frying
Caster sugar, for sprinkling
2 lemons, for serving

Makes about 10 pancakes

Sieve flour and salt together into a basin. Stir in lemon rind. Make a well in the centre and break in the egg. Beat well, incorporating the flour, and add half the liquid very gradually, beating all the time until a smooth batter is formed. Add remaining liquid a little at a time and beat until well mixed. Leave to stand for at least 30 minutes.

Stir melted butter into the batter just before cooking. Heat a very little butter in a pancake or omelet pan until very hot. Spoon in a tablespoon of batter and tip the pan until batter covers its base. Cook until golden brown underneath. Turn over with a palette knife and cook the other side until golden. Turn out on to sugared greaseproof paper, sprinkle with caster sugar and a squeeze of lemon juice. Serve immediately with extra sugar and lemon wedges, or keep warm in the oven until needed.

Variations

Orange Pancakes
Add grated rind of 2 oranges to the batter and cook in the usual way. To serve, sprinkle with sugar and pour orange juice over the pancakes.

Pancakes Ornate
Spread cooked pancakes with jam, roll up and serve with cream. Traditionally, apricot jam was used.

Caramelized Apple Pancakes
Fill cooked pancakes with apple slices sautéed in a little butter. Fold over and sprinkle generously with caster or icing sugar. Place under a hot grill just long enough to crisp the pancakes and glaze the sugar.

Sweet Apple Omelet

The ancestor of the British omelet, known as a 'herbolace', was a mixture of eggs and shredded herbs baked in a buttered dish. Cheese and milk were added later. This herbolace was replaced by the French 'omelette' in the 14th century, referred to in many English recipes as an 'aumelette' or 'alumelle', which gradually became omelet. The word 'omelette' probably came from the word derived from lamella *(Latin for a leaf or thin sheet). Even as late as the mid-17th century, opinions were still varied as to whether the omelet should be cooked on one side only or turned over and cooked on both sides, like a pancake. Eventually, the former way won although a hot 'salamander' or iron was sometimes held over the top of the omelet for a few seconds.*

The sweet omelet was very popular in Edwardian times and was often served as a country weekend treat, when the cook would prepare it while the guests were eating the main course. It would then be brought to the table, flaming with brandy or rum.

In this recipe the omelet is filled with apples, but you can use cherries, plums or apricots in the same way or just serve filled with jam which is the traditional way. Apricot jam was always used.

2 large cooking apples
115g (4oz) butter
115g (4oz) caster sugar
2 tablespoons apple brandy or rum

150ml (¼ pint) double or whipping cream
5 eggs
Pinch of salt

Serves 4

Peel, core and slice apples. Fry apples gently in 50g (1¾oz) butter, turning frequently until tender. Remove from heat and add 50g (1¾oz) caster sugar, apple brandy and double or whipping cream. Stir well. Separate 2 of the eggs and beat egg yolks and 3 whole eggs together. Add salt and 25g (1oz) caster sugar. Whisk the 2 egg whites until stiff and gently fold into egg mixture.

In a frying pan melt the remaining butter. When light brown in colour, pour in egg mixture and cook over a moderate heat, mixing it well with a fork to allow uncooked egg to run on to the bottom of the hot pan. Cook until golden brown on the bottom and cooked on the top (sweet omelets, unlike savoury omelets, should not be runny on the top). Spread apple mixture over the top, fold in half and slide on to a warmed plate. Sprinkle with remaining caster sugar and caramelize by placing the omelet under a very hot grill for a few minutes.

Another attractive way of finishing this omelet is to heat a skewer until it is red hot and then draw it over the top of the sugar-sprinkled omelet in a criss-cross pattern.

Puffed Strawberry Omelet

A fluffy sweet omelet flavoured with orange rind and orange flower water and filled with fresh strawberries. This kind of omelet was known as a popular treat over a hundred years ago.

3 eggs, separated
2 level teaspoons caster sugar
Grated rind of 1 orange
¼ teaspoon orange flower water (optional)
2 tablespoons water
15g (½oz) butter
225g (8oz) sliced strawberries
25g (1oz) icing sugar, sifted
1 tablespoon Grand Marnier (optional)

Serves 2

Whisk egg whites with caster sugar until stiff, but not dry. Beat egg yolks, orange rind, orange flower water, if using, and water until creamy. Melt butter in an omelet or small frying pan over a low heat. Fold egg whites carefully into yolks using a metal spoon. Be careful not to overmix. Tip omelet pan to coat sides with butter. Pour in egg mixture. Cook egg mixture over a moderate heat until golden brown underneath and just firm to touch in the centre. Place under pre-heated grill and cook until just set. Spread with sliced strawberries and sprinkle with sifted icing sugar. Fold omelet and slide gently on to a hot serving plate. Dredge with more icing sugar. Warm the Grand Marnier if using in a small saucepan, pour over omelet and set alight. Take to table immediately while omelet is still flaming. Serve with sweetened whipped cream.

Variation

A Puffed Lemon Omelet
Replace 1 tablespoon of the water with lemon juice, and use grated lemon rind instead of orange. Omit orange flower water and add a little more caster sugar. Serve without the strawberry filling. Set alight with brandy if you like.

Fruit and Jellies

New varieties of apple and pear were introduced from France in the middle ages. Other known garden or orchard fruit trees were plums, damsons, medlars, quinces and mulberries. Strange and exotic fruits like lemons, Seville oranges, pomegranates, raisins, currants, prunes, figs and dates had begun to arrive in Britain from southern Europe. These, particularly the dried fruits, were eaten in considerable quantities by the wealthy. The poor ate them on festive occasions, such as Christmas. Fresh fruit was regarded as bad for the digestion, so most fruits were roasted, baked or stewed in pottages.

The 16th century saw an upsurge of interest in fruit and fruit growing. Landowners began to take an interest in horticulture and their gardeners were kept busy developing new varieties of fruit and vegetables. Market gardening proved lucrative, especially around London, and Covent Garden was established as the City's fruit market. A wide range of fruits was being grown in southern and midland England. Further north, the climate imposed limitations and fruit was raised principally in the gardens of the gentry. There were parts of north-west England where even apples and plums were hardly known among ordinary people before the 18th century. In Scotland too, fruit was grown on a limited scale.

The medieval fear of uncooked fruit died hard and it was often blamed when a person fell ill suddenly. All through the 16th and 17th centuries, the best way to eat fruit was to cook it first with sugar and spices. Apples, pears (Wardens) and quinces were baked for several hours in pies. Soft fruits were boiled and pulped to form 'tartstuff' for pies and tarts or to be mixed with cream in a fool or similar creamy dish. These cooked fruits became an ingredient of puddings and were preserved so that they could be used all year round. It was only in the 18th century that fresh fruit began to be regarded as a safe and even healthy food, and its popularity has grown from strength to strength.

Jelly was particularly fashionable in the 17th century in making extremely decorative dishes and tableaux – fish swimming in ponds of jelly, birds flying in skies of jelly, great mounds of fresh fruit set in jelly and layers of almonds, raisins and candied fruits glistening through clear jelly. Usually they were highly coloured – even blue – and highly spiced. Wine jellies were very popular and later, jellies were flavoured with lemon juice, grape juice, bitter oranges or quinces. Jellies were stiffened originally with calves' feet or neatsfoot, later with hartshorn.

Black Caps

Apples were first baked in the ashes of the fire. The skins were often burnt on one side, hence the name Black Caps. Baked apples, frequently cooked in cider or wine, have continued to be a country favourite for centuries. They can be filled with any dried fruit and are delicious topped with honey, jam or marmalade.

The secret of a good baked apple is to use a quality cooking apple, preferably a Bramley, which is Britain's finest cooking apple. It was first grown in Nottinghamshire by an innkeeper and butcher called Matthew Bramley from Southwell, and introduced commercially in 1876. The Bramley is one of the late croppers and is large with a shiny green skin. It is very crisp and cooks superbly.

6 large Bramley cooking apples
50g (1¾oz) chopped dates
50g (1¾oz) sultanas
50g (1¾oz) raisins
25g (1oz) chopped almonds
 or hazelnuts
Grated rind and juice of 1 orange

85g (3oz) soft brown sugar
1 level teaspoon ground mace or
 mixed spice
40g (1½oz) butter
150ml (¼ pint) sweet sherry or
 Madeira

Serves 6

Wash and core apples. Score skin around the middle of each apple to prevent it bursting during baking, and stand close together in a well-buttered ovenproof dish. Mix chopped dates, sultanas, raisins and chopped nuts with orange rind and juice. Pack centres of apples with this mixture. Mix brown sugar and spice together and sprinkle over each apple. Top with a knob of butter. Pour sherry or Madeira around apples and bake in the centre of a preheated oven at 180°C, 350°F, gas mark 4 for 45–60 minutes, basting occasionally. Serve warm, topped with thick cream and/or Stem Ginger Ice Cream or Honey and Brandy Ice Cream (see pages 54 and 55) and extra brown sugar.

Variation

Iced Apples

Prepare as for Black Caps, but remove apples from oven about 15 minutes before end of the cooking time. Strip off the top half of the skin. Whisk 2 or 3 egg whites very stiffly and add 60–85g (2¼–3oz) caster sugar. Whisk again until stiff and glossy and then gently fold in another 60–85g (2¼–3oz) caster sugar. Coat baked apples with this meringue and return to the oven for a further 15 minutes, until meringue is crisp and lightly browned.

Cherries in Red Wine

900g (2lb) dark red cherries
25g (1oz) sugar
Pinch of ground cinnamon
150ml (¼ pint) red wine
3 tablespoons redcurrant jelly
Juice of 1 orange
1–1½ dessertspoons arrowroot
1–2 tablespoons cold water
3–4 sugar lumps
1 orange
300ml (½ pint) double cream

Serves 6

Stone cherries and place in a saucepan with the sugar and cinnamon. Cover pan and heat gently until the juices run freely, about 7–10 minutes. By this time the cherries will be at boiling point. Remove from heat, drain cherries and turn into a serving bowl, reserving juice. Put the wine in the saucepan and boil rapidly until reduced by half. Add the redcurrant jelly and orange juice and heat gently until the jelly has melted. Add the juice from the cherries. Dissolve 1 dessertspoon of arrowroot in 1 tablespoon of water and add this to the saucepan. Bring to boiling point again. The liquor should now be smooth and rich looking but not gluey. You may need more arrowroot – it really depends on the juiciness of your cherries. Pour juice over cherries and chill well.

Rub sugar lumps over the rind of the orange until they are orange-coloured and well impregnated. Crush them in a bowl and add the strained juice of the orange. Whip the cream lightly, until it will barely hold its shape. Fold in the orange syrup. Chill well. Serve separately or pour over the top of the cherries in their serving bowl. Decorate with orange rind and whole cherries.

Figs Baked in Wine

In the past, figs have been much more popular in British cookery than they are now. They were ripened in sheltered gardens in the south of England. There is something rather luxurious about fresh figs for pudding.

40g (1½oz) butter, at room temperature
12 fresh ripe figs
1½ teaspoons vanilla extract
115g (4oz) demerara sugar, or 4 tablespoons clear honey
100ml (3½fl oz) white wine
50ml (2fl oz) Marsala

Serves 4–6

Preheat the oven to 180°C, 350°F, gas mark 4. Smear the butter on a shallow ovenproof dish, large enough to hold all the figs snugly together. Wash and dry the figs, then cut a deep cross in the top, without cutting through them completely. Arrange them in the dish, sprinkle with vanilla extract and sugar, then pour the wine and Marsala around the figs.

Cover with foil and put on a high shelf in the oven for 20 minutes, then uncover and cook for a further 20 minutes.

Serve 2 figs per person with thick cream or Vanilla Ice Cream (see page 59) and the syrup drizzled around the dish.

Variation

Figs Baked in Claret
Bake figs in claret instead of white wine and substitute 2 tablespoons sugar for the honey.

Moonshine

This romantically named pudding is a lemony jelly, popular with 17th- and 18th-century cooks. Saffron would probably have been used to colour the jelly in the 17th century as highly coloured foods were extremely popular. Make it in a fancy Victorian mould if you have one.

115g (4oz) caster sugar
Finely pared rind of 2 lemons
600ml (1 pint) cold water
Juice of 2 lemons, strained
15g (½oz) gelatine

Serves 4–6

Put sugar, lemon rind and water in a saucepan. Bring to the boil and simmer for 15 minutes to allow lemon rind to infuse. Leave on one side to cool. Strain. Put strained lemon juice in a cup and sprinkle over gelatine. Place the cup in a pan of water and gently heat until the gelatine has melted. Strain through a warmed fine-mesh sieve into the cooled lemon syrup. Stir well to make sure gelatine is mixed in thoroughly. Leave to cool again and, when just beginning to set, whisk until jelly looks like snow. Turn into a wetted mould and refrigerate until set.

Turn out on to an attractive plate by dipping mould quickly in hot water. Serve chilled and decorated with a few small edible flowers and maidenhair fern, if you have a plant. Eat with homemade dessert biscuits.

Nectarines Baked in Cream

This delicious fruit has been known in Britain since the early 17th century and was frequently grown in the walled gardens of great houses. Peaches, pears and apricots are equally good in this recipe.

6 fresh nectarines
300ml (½ pint) double cream
115g (4oz) caster sugar
1 vanilla pod, split in half lengthways
25g (1oz) toasted flaked almonds

Serves 6

Skin nectarines by dropping in boiling water for a few minutes. Remove stones by running a knife round the fruit and twisting the two halves in opposite directions. Place nectarine halves in a shallow ovenproof dish. Heat cream, sugar and vanilla pod together gently until the sugar has dissolved. Pour cream over nectarines (don't remove vanilla pod). Bake in the centre of a moderate oven at 180°C, 350°F, gas mark 4 for 30–40 minutes or until the fruit is tender. Remove from oven and chill well. Serve very cold, sprinkled with toasted flaked almonds. This dish is also very good served with hot Easy Chocolate Sauce (see page 56) dribbled over the cream.

Variation

Creamy Nectarine Tart
Line a 30cm (12in) flan tin with shortcrust pastry. Bake blind for 10–15 minutes at 200°C, 400°F, gas mark 6 (see Apricot Amber Pudding, page 17, for instructions on baking blind). Fill cooked pastry case with nectarine mixture as above and bake for a further 30 minutes.

Brandied Peaches

Peaches were introduced by the Romans and by the 17th century there were 22 varieties growing in Britain. Recipes for brandied fruit, one of the early ways of preserving, began to appear at the beginning of the 18th century. Peaches, nectarines, apricots, cherries and grapes were packed into earthenware jars containing brandy and a little sugar syrup. The jars were sealed closely and the fruit was ready for future use.

6 fresh peaches
Boiling water to cover peaches
Juice of 1 lemon
12 cloves
300ml (½ pint) cold water
115g (4oz) granulated sugar
5cm (2in) piece of cinnamon stick
1 bay leaf
25g (1oz) butter
2 tablespoons brandy

Serves 6

Cover peaches with boiling water for about 2 minutes. Remove from the water, and skin. Halve and stone peaches. Brush all over with lemon juice to stop them discolouring. Stick a clove in each half. Put water, sugar, cinnamon stick, bay leaf and butter into a small saucepan. Bring slowly to the boil to dissolve sugar. When it has completely dissolved, boil for 5 minutes to make a sugar syrup. Place peaches in a shallow ovenproof dish. Add brandy to sugar syrup and pour over peaches. Cover and bake in the centre of a preheated oven at 160°C, 325°F, gas mark 3 for about 30 minutes, or until peaches are tender, but still hold their shape. Remove bay leaf and cinnamon stick and serve either hot or cold with whipped cream.

Spiced Pears in Red Wine.

The earliest pears were called 'wardens' and were extremely hard. Many recipes like this were devised for cooking them slowly for several hours until they softened. Cider, or sweet white wine, can replace red wine

4 large, good-shaped hard pears with stalks
300ml (½ pint) red wine
85g (3oz) caster sugar
1 vanilla pod, split in half lengthways
1 small cinnamon stick
4 cloves
Zest of 1 orange
1 thick slice of fresh ginger, peeled
1 rounded teaspoon arrowroot

Serves 4

Preheat the oven to 130°C, 250°F, gas mark ½. Peel the pears thinly with a potato peeler leaving the stalks intact. Remove the 'eyes' opposite the stalk ends and cut a thin slice from the bottom of each pear so that they stand upright easily. Lay the pears on their side in a flameproof casserole dish with a tight-fitting lid.

Pour over the wine and sprinkle over the sugar. Scrape the seeds out of the vanilla pod and add to the casserole with the pod, cinnamon stick, cloves, orange zest and ginger.

Bring everything up to simmering point, then cover the casserole and bake on a low shelf in the oven for about 1½ hours, then turn the pears on to their other side and cook for a further 1½ hours. When the pears are cooked, carefully lift them out with a slotted spoon, standing them upright in a dish.
Strain the cooking liquor into a bowl, then pour back into the casserole. Place over direct heat. Mix the arrowroot to a smooth paste, with a little cold water, then add to the wine mixture, whisking all the time. Bring just up to simmering point when the liquor will have thickened. Remove from the heat and cool.

Spoon over the pears when cool and baste well. Cover the dish with foil and chill thoroughly in the refrigerator, basting frequently, with the wine sauce. Serve bathed in the sauce, with Vanilla Ice Cream (see page 59) or thick cream.

Pears in Nightshirts

The combination of apples and pears is a very old one, as they were the first two fruits to be grown in Britain. For this recipe, the pears are poached in cider, set on a bed of apple pulp and coated with crisp, pale brown meringue – 'the nightshirts'.

6 large firm dessert pears
425ml (¾ pint) cider
700g (1lb 9oz) cooking apples
15g (½oz) butter
Grated rind of 1 lemon
1 tablespoon lemon juice
2–3 cloves
85g–115g (3–4oz) caster sugar
85g (3oz) icing sugar, sifted
6 egg whites
Pinch of salt
350g (12oz) caster sugar
50g (1¾oz) toasted flaked almonds

Serves 6

Peel pears, but leave on the stalks. Put the cider into a saucepan large enough to take the pears. Bring to the boil and lower pears gently into this liquor. Cover and simmer very gently for 30–35 minutes or until pears are translucent and just tender.

While pears are cooking, make apple pulp. Peel, core and slice apples. Rub butter over the sides and the bottom of a saucepan. Add apple slices, lemon rind, lemon juice and cloves. Cover with buttered greaseproof paper and cook over a low heat for about 15 minutes until apples are soft and any liquid has evaporated. Stir gently from time to time. Remove cloves and beat the apples to a smooth thick pulp with a wooden spoon. Add sugar to taste. Pour into a buttered ovenproof dish large enough to take the pears, allowing room for meringue coating.

Drain cooked pears and roll each one in sifted icing sugar. Place pears on top of apple pulp. Whisk egg whites until very stiff. Add 175g (6oz) caster sugar and whisk until stiff and glossy. Fold in remaining 175g (6oz) caster sugar and spread or pipe a thick coating of meringue over pears. Bake in a preheated oven at 200°C, 400°F, gas mark 6 for 10–15 minutes or until meringue is crisp and light brown. Serve immediately, sprinkled with toasted flaked almonds.

Baked Quinces in Cinnamon Syrup

*Quinces have been grown in Britain since Anglo-Saxon times, when they were probably eaten stewed with honey. The first marmalade to arrive here in medieval days from southern Europe was made from the fruit (*marmelo* is Portuguese for 'quince') and in Elizabethan times the fruit was particularly highly regarded. So we have had a long love affair with the quince – and hurray, it is back in fashion. If you have room in your garden, plant an old-fashioned quince tree – it is a thing of beauty all year round.*

The quince needs long, slow cooking to turn its dry pale yellow flesh into an extraordinary deep pinky-red succulent delight, but it's worth the effort. The sweet, musky perfume given off is indescribable.

6 quinces
Juice of 2 lemons
200g (7oz) caster sugar
1 vanilla pod, split in half lengthways
About 300ml (½ pint) water
1 small stick of cinnamon
4 cloves

Serves 4

Peel 4 of the quinces and cut into quarters. Remove the cores and place in a large heavy lidded ovenproof dish, arranging the fruit in a single layer. Pour over the lemon juice to prevent discolouration.

Use the remaining 2 quinces to make the syrup. Peel, core and chop them coarsely, then place in a pan with half the sugar and the vanilla pod seeds. Add enough water to cover. Bring to the boil and simmer for about 1 hour, or until the quinces are very soft and the liquid has turned syrupy. Strain and discard the quince pulp.

Pour the syrup over the prepared quince quarters, adding the cinnamon, cloves and remaining sugar. Make sure the quinces are covered by the syrup, adding a little more water if necessary. Place a piece of greaseproof paper on top to keep the fruit submerged.

Cover with the lid of the pan and place in a preheated oven at 130°C, 250°F, gas mark ½ and cook for 2–3 hours, or until the quinces are soft to touch and golden in colour.

Serve warm with either Vanilla Custard Sauce, Honey and Brandy Ice Cream, Vanilla Ice Cream (see pages 29, 55 and 59) or with thick cream.

Right: Baked Quinces in Cinnamon Syrup
Next page: Pears in Nightshirts

Rhubarb and Red Wine Jelly

An ideal pudding, after a rich meal. Use young, pink, forced, rhubarb for the best colour and flavour.

450g (1lb) young or forced rhubarb
5cm (2in) piece of fresh ginger
150g (5½oz) cane sugar
Juice of 2 lemons
Juice of 2 oranges
850ml (1½ pints) red wine
4 tablespoons water
40g (1½oz) gelatine

Serves 6–8

Cut the rhubarb into 2.5cm (1in) pieces and place in a large pan with the peeled and roughly chopped ginger. Add the sugar and strain the lemon and orange juices into the mixture through a fine sieve, then add the wine.

Set the pan over the heat, bring to the boil, then simmer gently for about 15 minutes, or until the rhubarb is completely mushy. Remove the pan from the heat and strain the liquid through the finest sieve into another bowl or a clean pan. Don't press the rhubarb against the sieve, or the juices will become cloudy.

Put the 4 tablespoons of water into a small pan, bring to bubbling point and remove from the heat. Sprinkle over the gelatine and stir until completely dissolved. Pass through a sieve into the rhubarb and wine liquor, then pour into a 1.3 litre (2¼ pint) jelly mould. Leave until cold, then transfer to the refrigerator to set.

Just before serving, dip the mould in hot water for a few seconds, then turn the jelly out on to a cake stand or serving plate, giving it a good shake to release it. Decorate with primroses, or other edible spring flowers and serve with cream.

Left: Rhubarb and Red Wine Jelly
Previous page: Clare College Mush

Clare College Mush

*Also called Eton Mess, the original recipe for this traditional pudding is said to have come
from Clare College, Cambridge. A delicious combination of strawberries, cream and crushed
meringues, it can be flavoured with an orange or berry liqueur or vanilla. Other fruits work
well – raspberries, and poached apricots, rhubarb, damsons and plums are favourites, but
best of all I like a combination of strawberries and raspberries with a flavouring of liqueur
and half cream and half yoghurt.*

2 large egg whites
50g (2oz) caster sugar
50g (2oz) icing sugar
225g (8oz) fresh strawberries
225g (8oz) fresh raspberries
1 tablespoon (plus an extra dash) raspberry liqueur
200ml (7fl oz) double cream
200ml (7fl oz) natural yoghurt

Serves 6

Preheat the oven to 100°C, 200°F, gas mark ¼. Whisk the egg whites until they form soft peaks, then
beat in the caster sugar a little at a time. Continue whisking for a further 10 minutes until the mix is
smooth and shiny, then sift in the icing sugar. Spoon on to non-stick baking paper arranged on a baking
tray, then bake in the oven until dry, but with a slightly soft, chewy centre – about 2 hours. Remove
from the oven and leave to cool on a wire rack.

When ready to assemble the pudding – and it is best eaten within 2 hours of making – cut the
strawberries into halves or quarters, depending on their size, then toss with a dash of raspberry
liqueur. Stir in the raspberries, reserving a few of the best for decoration.

Lightly whip the cream and yoghurt with a tablespoon of raspberry liqueur. Break the meringues
into walnut-sized pieces and gently stir into the cream mixture with the fruit (don't overmix, because
it looks best with a raspberry-ripple effect).

Spoon into glass dishes and serve chilled, decorated with the reserved raspberries.

Summer Pudding

The true old-fashioned Summer Pudding was made with raspberries and redcurrants only, but if you wish, you can include small halved strawberries, white currants, blueberries, sweet, firm-fleshed cherries and a few blackcurrants – not many of the latter or they will dominate the pudding. If you are lucky enough to be able to get hold of some mulberries, they make a delicious summer pudding, combined with half the amount of strawberries. Make sure you use good-quality bread.

700g (1lb 9oz) fresh raspberries
200g (7oz) fresh redcurrants
115g (4oz) vanilla caster sugar or
 plain caster sugar

About 6 slices of day-old white bread
 about 8mm (⅜in) thick
2 tablespoons raspberry liqueur

Serves 6

Put the fruit into a heavy saucepan and sprinkle over the sugar. Heat gently for 3–4 minutes only, until the sugar has dissolved and the juices have begun to flow. Cut the crusts off the bread and use it to line an 850ml (1½ pint) pudding basin, bottom and sides. Overlap the slices slightly so that there are no gaps. Spoon the fruit into the basin, reserving a little of the juice for serving. Pour the raspberry liqueur over the fruit before finishing with a top layer of bread.

Put a plate on top that fits exactly inside the basin and weight it fairly heavily. Leave the pudding in the refrigerator overnight. Turn out just before serving and pour the reserved juice over any bread that isn't quite soaked through. Serve chilled with pouring cream or softly whipped double cream.

Variation

Spiced Winter Pudding

Soak 175g (6oz) dried apricots in 600ml (1 pint) water overnight. Place the apricots and soaking liquor in a saucepan and bring to boil. Simmer uncovered for 10–15 minutes. Strain apricots, reserving liquor. Return 300ml (½ pint) of liquor to saucepan with 350g (12oz) peeled, cored and sliced cooking apples, 50g (1¾oz) raisins and 1 level teaspoon ground cinnamon. Cook until apples are soft. Add apricots. Put 2 tablespoons warm water in a cup and sprinkle over 15g (½oz) gelatine. Place cup in a small saucepan of hot water and heat gently to dissolve agent. Pour through a warmed fine-mesh sieve into the fruit mixture (this ensures that any tiny lumps are removed. If the sieve is not warm, a thin layer of gelatine will remain on it and then your proportions will be wrong). Add 115–175g (4–6oz) caster sugar to taste and leave to cool a little. Line and fill the basin as described above. Just before serving, unmould and decorate with whipped cream and raisins. Serve very cold.

Plums in Sloe Gin

Large Victoria plums have the best flavour for this dish, so make the most of them when they are in season.

900g (2lb) firm, but ripe, plums
115g (4oz) soft brown sugar
1 teaspoon vanilla extract
200ml (7fl oz) sloe gin, homemade or bought

Serves 4–6

Preheat the oven to 180°C, 350°F, gas mark 4. Halve and stone the plums, then place them in one layer in a large shallow ovenproof dish. Sprinkle with the sugar.

Stir the vanilla extract into the sloe gin and pour over the plums. Cover tightly with foil and place in the oven for about 45 minutes. Baste the plums once during this time, taking care not to break them up. The plums should be cooked, but not falling apart and sitting in a puddle of gloriously boozy crimson syrup.

Serve the plums barely warm, or at room temperature, with their juices and some thick cream.

Port Wine Jelly

This posh jelly makes a very good alternative to plum pudding for Christmas lunch.

300ml (½ pint) cold water
115g (4oz) cane sugar, preferably cube
1 tablespoon redcurrant jelly
2.5cm (1in) piece of cinnamon stick
3 cloves
1 bay leaf
Grated rind of 1 lemon
1 blade of mace
300ml (½ pint) ruby port
1 tablespoon brandy
15g (½oz) gelatine

Serves 6

Place cold water, sugar, redcurrant jelly, cinnamon stick, cloves, bay leaf, lemon rind and mace in a clean saucepan over gentle heat, stirring occasionally. When the sugar has completely dissolved and the jelly has melted, bring to the boil. Simmer for 10 minutes.

Put port and brandy into a second clean saucepan and heat gently. Sprinkle on the gelatine and bring to the boil. Simmer for 10 minutes. Strain contents of both saucepans through a fine sieve into a large jug, stir, and as jelly cools pour into 6 stemmed glass dishes. Leave to set in the refrigerator.

Serve chilled with pouring cream and homemade shortbread.

Milk Puddings, Custards and Trifles

Milk puddings were developed from the cereal pottages of medieval times. The new cereal of the later medieval period was rice imported from Italy on the spice ships and this, alongside sweetened milk pottages of crumbled bread, barley, oatmeal and wheat, was eaten on fasting days – the milk used was from almonds as milk from animals was forbidden.

Until the 17th century milk pottages continued to be eaten on fasting days only, but eventually rice and sago puddings were accepted as supper dishes among the gentry. Milk puddings tended to be elaborate affairs and were highly flavoured with spices, rose water or orange flower water. In Georgian times milk puddings were often baked in a pastry case and were rich with cream, eggs and dried fruit. Sometimes they were boiled in a well-buttered cloth instead of being baked.

The Elizabethans were particularly fond of custard. It was usually served in a crust or mould of paste like our present-day custard pies and tarts. A favourite Elizabethan joke was 'The Almaine Leap into a Custard': a jester suddenly entered the room where a meal was taking place and, springing over the heads of the astounded guests, plunged himself into an enormous dish of custard placed on the table. This joke was popular at the Lord Mayor's feast in London.

There are two types of custard: baked or steamed, and the softer pouring custard, which is used as a sauce. Egg whites set a baked custard and egg yolks give it a creamy consistency, but as the yolks thicken at a higher temperature than the whites, it is important to cook custards at the correct temperature. Too much heat, especially direct heat, will curdle an egg custard, so use a double saucepan, if you have one, for making a custard sauce, and stand a baked custard in a roasting tin half-filled with cold water. If you haven't a double saucepan, use a heavy-based saucepan with a film of cold water in the bottom over very gentle heat. Using a little cornflour in a custard sauce helps to prevent it curdling and, if the worst should happen, a curdled custard can often be rescued by turning it into a cold bowl and whisking quickly. Sieving will also help.

The original trifle of the Tudor and Stuart period was very different from our modern-day version. It was just thick cream heated until lukewarm with spices, usually ginger, sugar and rose water. By 1751, trifle was being made with crumbled Naples biscuits, macaroons and ratafias soaked in sack (sweet sherry) at the bottom of the bowl, and these were covered with a rich custard and topped with syllabub. Later recipes replaced the syllabub with whipped or 'milled' cream, fruit or preserve was included and the modern trifle was established.

Fine Almond Blancmange

Although its actual name is undoubtedly of French origin, blancmange has been known in Britain for many centuries. It is mentioned in some of the oldest cookery books as 'blewe manger' or 'blank mange' or 'white food'. Chaucer, in The Canterbury Tales, *describes it as a mixture of 'minced capon with flour, cream and sugar'. In fact, it was made with any white meat stewed with rice, dried fruits, almonds and spices. Exactly when the meat was omitted is not known, but by Elizabethan times the dish had become a mixture of cream, sugar and rose water, thickened with egg yolks.*

The English blancmange of the 18th century was a kind of jelly, stiffened with isinglass or hartshorn and flavoured with almonds and rose water. By the early 1820s, arrowroot was being exported to Britain from the West Indies and became the thickening agent. Boiling milk, sweetened and seasoned with cinnamon, mace, and lemon peel, was poured on to a solution of arrowroot. It was set in elaborate moulds – and here was the true forerunner of our modern cornflour blancmange.

Try experimenting with different flavourings like chocolate, coffee, lemon, orange, brandy or other liqueurs, and vanilla.

40g (1½oz) cornflour
300ml (½ pint) milk
300ml (½ pint) single cream
1 bay leaf
Strip of lemon peel
2 tablespoons caster sugar
4–5 drops almond essence
25g (1oz) toasted flaked almonds

Serves 4–6

Mix the cornflour to a smooth paste with a little of the milk. Heat the rest of the milk and cream in a saucepan with the bay leaf and lemon peel and gradually blend in cornflour mixture. Bring to simmering point and cook for about 3 minutes, stirring continuously until thickened. Remove from heat and sweeten to taste. Stir in almond essence. Pour into a fancy 600ml (1 pint) mould, rinsed out with cold water. Put in refrigerator to set. Unmould on to a plate, decorate with toasted almonds and serve with fresh soft fruit or a fruit sauce and pouring cream or yoghurt.

Spicy Ground Rice Pudding

This recipe is based on one by Eliza Acton, one of the best known of the 19th-century cookery writers. Eggs are added to make a richer pudding. Pies and puddings were often 'iced' or topped with egg whites as in this recipe.

40g (1½oz) ground rice or semolina
600ml (1 pint) full-cream milk
Strip of lemon peel
1 vanilla pod
1 bay leaf
Pinch of ground nutmeg
25g (1oz) caster sugar or ½ tablespoon honey
2 eggs, separated
25g (1oz) butter
Grated nutmeg or ground cinnamon for sprinkling
115g (4oz) caster sugar

Serves 4–6

Butter thoroughly a 1.2 litre (2 pint) ovenproof dish. Mix ground rice or semolina to a smooth paste with a little of the milk in a basin. Boil the rest of the milk with the lemon peel, vanilla pod, bay leaf and pinch of nutmeg. Pour on to ground rice or semolina, stirring continuously. Rinse the pan in which the milk was boiled and leave a film of cold water on the bottom. Return rice and milk and bring slowly to the boil again, stirring all the time, so that it does not burn on the bottom of the saucepan. Cook gently for 10 minutes. Add the sugar or honey. Beat egg yolks and beat into rice. Remove vanilla pod, bay leaf and lemon peel. Pour into prepared pie dish. Dot with butter and sprinkle with nutmeg or cinnamon. Bake in the centre of a preheated oven at 180°C, 350°F, gas mark 4 for about 25 minutes. Whisk egg whites until stiff and whisk in 50g (1¾oz) caster sugar. Fold in the remaining caster sugar. Pile the sweetened egg whites on top of the pudding and bake for a further 20 minutes until meringue is crisp and lightly browned. Serve hot with pouring cream and a fruit sauce.

Variation

Try edging pie dish with puff pastry, or adding 50g (1¾oz) currants, sultanas or raisins and 25g (1oz) candied peel.

Old-fashioned Rice Pudding

In Georgian times a rice pudding could be a very elaborate dish. It was either tied loosely in a cloth, boiled and eaten with melted butter, sugar or salt, or a richer dish including eggs, cream, butter, marrow, currants, brandy, ratafia, nutmeg and candied peel was baked with 'a paste round the edge'. You can flavour your pudding with lemon or orange rind, ground cinnamon or nutmeg, ½ vanilla pod (split lengthways), a few drops of rose water, a few saffron threads or 1 fresh bay leaf. The important thing is to cook the rice very slowly if it is to achieve that unctuous richness and a buttery brown crust. If you have an Aga or similar stove, leave it in the lowest oven overnight, though you will need to add more milk.

55g (2oz) short-grain rice
850ml (1½ pints) full-cream milk
25g (1oz) butter, cut into little pieces
55g (2oz) caster sugar or 1 level tablespoon clear honey or golden syrup
Pinch of salt
1 curl of lemon rind
150ml (¼ pint) double cream
Freshly grated nutmeg

Serves 4–6

Put the rice, milk, butter, sugar, salt and lemon rind into a buttered ovenproof dish. Stir well, then add the cream. Stir again, then grate over plenty of nutmeg. Place uncovered in a preheated slow oven at 140°C, 275°F, gas mark 1 and cook for 3–4 hours, or until just starting to set. As the pudding cools, it will finish cooking in its own heat and thicken. Remove from oven and leave until just warm, or cold, if you like.

Serve on its own, or with Jam, Marmalade or Syrup Sauce (see pages 92, 155 and 156) or with stewed or fresh fruit.

Variations

Try adding 50g (1¾oz) chopped natural glacé cherries, candied peel, sultanas, currants or grated apple.

Rice Pudding Meringue
Make a meringue topping with 2 egg whites and 115g (4oz) caster sugar. Pile on top of the rice pudding and return to the oven to brown the meringue.

Rice Creams

This delicate creamy pudding can be served with fresh soft fruit or any fruit sauce. It is basically a cold rice pudding, mixed with cream, but this description doesn't do it justice.

60g (2oz) short-grain rice
300ml (½ pint) full-cream milk
25g (1oz) caster sugar
1 vanilla pod
1 bay leaf
1 level teaspoon gelatine
2 eggs, separated
300ml (½ pint) double or whipping cream

Serves 4–6

Wash the rice in cold water, drain and put in a heavy saucepan with the milk, sugar, vanilla pod and bay leaf. Bring slowly to the boil, then cook over gentle heat, stirring now and again to stop rice sticking on the bottom of the pan, until tender, about 40–45 minutes.

Remove from heat and take out vanilla pod and bay leaf. Sprinkle the gelatine into the hot rice and stir until dissolved. Beat egg yolks with 1 tablespoon cream and stir into rice. Return the pan to the heat for a few minutes, and then place in a bowl of cold water. Stir until cool, but not set.

Whip remainder of the cream, until it begins to ribbon but does not stand in peaks. Whisk egg whites until very stiff. Fold cream into cool rice, followed by egg whites. Pour into individual glasses and chill before serving. Decorate with a few raspberries or strawberries and place glasses on saucers covered with a fern leaf or strawberry leaves.

Durham Fluffin'

A milk pudding traditionally eaten in the north-east of England on Christmas Eve. The pearl barley has to be soaked in water overnight.

2 tablespoons pearl barley, soaked overnight in water
600ml (1 pint) full-cream milk
¾ teaspoon grated nutmeg
A few drops of brandy
50g (1¾oz) soft brown sugar or 1 tablespoon honey
Crystallized orange slices for decorating

Serves 6

Simmer soaked pearl barley in the milk for about 30 minutes or until it is a smooth cream. Add grated nutmeg, brandy, and sugar or honey to taste. Serve hot in individual dishes with plenty of pouring cream, decorated with crystallized orange slices or with cream and Jam Sauce (see below).

Jam Sauce

3 tablespoons raspberry, strawberry, plum, apricot or blackcurrant jam
6 tablespoons water
1 teaspoon lemon juice

Melt the jam in a saucepan with water and lemon juice. Push through a sieve to make a smooth sauce. Serve hot.

Caramel Pudding

This is a very elegant pudding which appeals to even the most jaded of appetites. The custard pudding is covered with a beautiful caramel sauce, and is delicious served with fresh strawberries or raspberries. Try flavouring with orange rind and juice instead of brandy.

115g (4oz) lump sugar
4 tablespoons cold water
1 teaspoon boiling water
600ml (1 pint) full-cream milk
1 vanilla pod
1 bay leaf
2 eggs
3 egg yolks
2 tablespoons caster sugar
1 tablespoon brandy (optional)

Serves 6

Preheat the oven to 160°C, 325°F, gas mark 3. Warm a 15cm (6in) souffle dish, or a 15cm (6in) cake tin or a fluted mould (this makes a very attractive pudding) in the oven. You can also use individual moulds.

Put sugar and cold water in a heavy-based saucepan. Heat gently until the sugar has dissolved. Bring to the boil and boil rapidly without stirring until a rich brown caramel is formed. Remove from heat, add boiling water and pour into warmed dish or mould. Using oven gloves or a tea towel, tip mould carefully to coat the bottom and sides with hot caramel. Leave to get cold.

Heat the milk with the vanilla pod and bay leaf. Leave to stand for 30 minutes to infuse. Bring to the boil and remove vanilla pod and bay leaf. Beat eggs, egg yolks and sugar together until pale in colour. Pour cooled milk on to egg mixture a little at a time to avoid curdling eggs, stirring continuously. Stir in brandy, if using. Strain custard into prepared mould. Stand in a roasting tin half-filled with hot water and bake in the centre of a preheated oven for about 45 minutes (30 minutes for individual moulds) or until custard is set. Cooking time will vary depending on the mould you have chosen.

When cooked, remove pudding from the oven, leave to cool completely and refrigerate before unmoulding. To unmould, loosen the edges of the pudding with the point of a knife. Place a shallow serving dish over mould and turn out quickly. Serve chilled with soft fruit.

Queen Mab's Pudding

This pudding is based on a recipe by Eliza Acton, from her Modern Cookery, *published in 1845. It is really a custard, set with gelatine, with candied fruits added to make it richer. Candying was a method of preserving fruit, popular in Tudor and Stuart days. Whole fruits were candied and served at the banquet course after the main meal, as well as being chopped and used in cakes, puddings and biscuits. If possible buy whole candied peel and chop it yourself.*

600ml (1 pint) full-cream milk
1 bay leaf
1 vanilla pod
Strip of lemon peel
2 large eggs, separated
40g (1½oz) caster sugar
2 tablespoons warm water
15g (½oz) gelatine
50g (1¾oz) chopped glacé cherries
25g (1oz) chopped candied citron or lemon peel

Serves 4–6

Put milk, bay leaf, vanilla pod and lemon peel in a saucepan and bring slowly to the boil. Remove from heat and cool a little. Beat egg yolks and sugar together and pour on flavoured milk, stirring continuously. Remove bay leaf, vanilla pod and lemon peel. Rinse milk pan with cold water, leaving a film of water on the bottom, and return milk and egg mixture to pan. Heat gently, stirring all the time and cook until thick enough to coat the back of a wooden spoon. Remove from heat.

Put warm water in a cup and sprinkle over gelatine. Place the cup in a pan of water and heat gently until the gelatine has dissolved. Pour through a warmed fine-mesh sieve into the custard. Whisk egg whites very stiffly and fold into cooled custard. Pour into a wetted mould and leave in a cool place until almost set. Stir in chopped cherries and peel and refrigerate to set completely. Serve with a fruit sauce poured around pudding.

Queen's Pudding

Also called Queen of Puddings, it was named after Queen Victoria and was created by her chefs at Buckingham Palace, but it was, in fact, based on a much older 17th-century recipe – a milk pudding thickened with breadcrumbs and eggs. It was originally baked in a 'puff paste' case. Try using lemon or lime curd instead of jam.

85g (3oz) fresh white breadcrumbs
3 eggs, separated
200g (7oz) caster sugar
600ml (1 pint) full-cream milk
25g (1oz) butter
Grated rind of ½ lemon
3 tablespoons raspberry jam

Serves 6

Butter a 1.2 litre (2 pint) ovenproof dish. Sprinkle breadcrumbs in the bottom of the dish. Beat egg yolks with 25g (1oz) caster sugar. Put milk, butter and grated lemon rind into a saucepan and bring slowly to the boil. Leave to cool a little and then pour on to egg yolks, stirring continuously until mixture is smooth. Strain the custard over breadcrumbs and leave to soak for at least 15 minutes. Stand dish in a roasting tin half-filled with hot water and bake in the centre of a preheated oven at 180°C, 350°F, gas mark 4 for 25–30 minutes, or until lightly set. Warm the jam and spread over the top of the pudding. Whisk egg whites until very stiff and add 85g (3oz) caster sugar. Whisk again until stiff and glossy. Fold in remaining sugar. Pile or pipe meringue on top of jam. Sprinkle with extra sugar and bake for a further 15–20 minutes or until meringue is crisp and lightly browned.

Serve warm, with or without Jam Sauce (see page 92) and pouring cream, or cold with fresh raspberries and cream.

Variation

Manchester Pudding
Put a layer of apricot jam in the bottom of an ovenproof dish. Continue as before, but include 2 tablespoons sherry or brandy in the custard. When the pudding is lightly set, spread with more apricot jam, and top with meringue as before. Serve warm or cold with pouring cream and poached fresh apricots.

Devonshire Junket

This was a junket covered with clotted cream, popular in Devon and Cornwall – so simple, but so delicious. Junket has been made since the 13th century and is probably of Norman origin. Its name comes from the word jonquette, *French for the little rush baskets in which it was made. The original junket was a rich confection of cream, curdled with rennet and flavoured with spices. Later, rose water and orange flower water were added and junket was eaten alongside the jellies and flummeries at the end of a meal. It was traditionally served in beautiful junket bowls with stewed fruit, but is especially good with fresh raspberries or strawberries.*

**600ml (1 pint) Jersey milk
  or single cream**
1 heaped tablespoon caster sugar
1 tablespoon brandy

Pinch of freshly grated nutmeg
1 level teaspoon rennet
Extra freshly grated nutmeg
Clotted cream, to serve

Serves 4

Heat the milk or cream to 39°C (100°F). Stir in the sugar to dissolve it, followed by the brandy, nutmeg and rennet. Stir well, then pour into a glass bowl or 4 individual serving dishes and leave to set at room temperature (not in the refrigerator), for about 4 hours.

Chill in the refrigerator for about 1 hour before serving plain or sprinkled with grated nutmeg and accompanied by clotted cream and soft fruit or purée of raspberries or strawberries.

Variation

Orange or Lemon Junket
Flavour the milk with the grated rind of 1 orange or lemon.

Damask Cream
For a junket popular in 18th-century Bath, make the junket using single cream rather than milk and omitting the brandy. Sprinkle with grated nutmeg. About 30 minutes before serving, mix together 4 tablespoons double or whipping cream, 3 tablespoons rose water and 1 tablespoon caster sugar. Pour this over the top of the junket. Serve with pink or red rose petals strewn over the top. Alternatively mix 4 tablespoons clotted cream with the rose water and sugar and serve separately with the junket.

Right: Devonshire Junket
Next page: Queen's Pudding

Floating Islands

This Georgian pudding consists of a rich custard covered with poached meringues (the islands).

600ml (1 pint) single cream
6 egg yolks
2 level teaspoons cornflour
175g (6oz) caster sugar
1 tablespoon rose water
850ml (1½ pints) milk, for poaching

1 vanilla pod
4 egg whites
Pinch of salt
Crystallized rose petals
Toasted flaked almonds

Serves 6–8

Bring cream gently to the boil in a heavy saucepan. Remove from heat and cool a little. Cream egg yolks, cornflour and 50g (1¾oz) sugar until almost white. Pour hot cream over egg yolk mixture gradually, beating all the time. Rinse out the saucepan leaving a film of cold water on the bottom. Return custard to the saucepan and heat gently, stirring continuously until thick enough to coat the back of a wooden spoon (don't boil or the mixture will curdle). Remove from heat and cool a little before stirring in rose water. Strain into a shallow serving bowl, sprinkle with sugar and leave to cool.

To make the 'islands', fill a frying pan with milk, flavoured with a vanilla pod, and bring to simmering point. Whisk egg whites with a pinch of salt until stiff peaks. Whisk in 115g (4oz) caster sugar gradually, until smooth and shiny. Remove vanilla pod from the pan. Using a tablespoon rinsed in cold water between each addition, spoon 4 islands into the pan of simmering water. Poach on each side for 2–3 minutes, until firm. Remove each island and drain on a clean towel. Repeat until meringue mixture is used up (about 8 islands). Leave to cool. Arrange islands on the 'lake' of custard and chill. To serve, sprinkle with crushed crystallized rose petals and toasted flaked almonds.

Variation

Caramel Floating Islands
Make as above, but decorate with caramel. Heat 50g (1¾oz) caster sugar in a small saucepan with 2 tablespoons cold water until dissolved, then raise the temperature and cook without stirring until it becomes a rich, golden caramel. Drizzle fine lines of the caramel in a crisscross design onto sheets of baking paper and set aside to cool. When serving, break off pieces and lay on top of the meringues.

Left: Floating Islands
Previous page: Apple and Brandy Trifle

Apple and Brandy Trifle

FOR THE BASE
1 fatless sponge made with 3 eggs, 85g
(3oz) caster sugar, 85g (3oz) plain
flour or 1 packet trifle sponges
About 6 tablespoons apple brandy

FOR THE APPLE LAYER
3 large Bramley apples
3 Cox's apples
2 tablespoons light soft brown sugar
½ teaspoon ground cinnamon

FOR THE CUSTARD
425ml (¾ pint) double cream
1 vanilla pod, split in half lengthways
2 large eggs
2 large egg yolks
85g (3oz) caster sugar

FOR THE CREAM TOPPING
300ml (½ pint) double cream
25g (1oz) icing sugar
Vanilla extract to taste

FOR DECORATION
100g (3½oz) flaked almonds
25g (1oz) icing sugar
3 tablespoons apple brandy

Serves 6–8

Cut the sponge into 2.5cm (1in) slices and arrange in a large bowl. Pour over the apple brandy and leave for at least 30 minutes to soak in. To make the apple layer, peel, core and roughly chop the apples. Place in a saucepan with the sugar and cinnamon. Cook over a medium heat until the apples are tender, then set aside to cool.

To make the custard, pour the double cream into a saucepan with the vanilla pod and bring to the boil. Meanwhile, mix the eggs, egg yolks and sugar together in a large bowl. When the cream reaches boiling point, pour it over the egg mixture, whisking continuously to prevent the eggs from curdling. Strain through a fine sieve into a large bowl. Place over a pan of simmering water. Heat until the custard has thickened, whisking from time to time. Set aside to cool. Cover the soaked sponge with a layer of the apple mixture, then a layer of custard.

For the cream topping, whisk together the cream, icing sugar and vanilla until it forms soft peaks. Spoon on top of the custard layer.

Mix the almonds, icing sugar and apple brandy together in a small bowl. Tip out on to a baking tray and toast in a preheated oven at 180°C, 350°F, gas mark 4 for 15 minutes, or until golden brown. Leave to cool, then scatter over the cream to decorate.

Mrs Beeton's Gooseberry Trifle

In this recipe, gooseberry pulp has replaced the more usual sponge cake at the bottom of the trifle, and is covered with a rich custard and topped with a 'whip' which was a Victorian version of syllabub. If possible, make the syllabub topping a day in advance. Any fruit pulp can be used.

Grated rind and juice of 1 lemon
6 tablespoons sweet white wine or sherry
2 tablespoons brandy
50g (1¾oz) caster sugar
600ml (1 pint) double cream
700g (1lb 9oz) green gooseberries
3 tablespoons cold water
250g (9oz) caster sugar
Strip of lemon peel
4 egg yolks
1 level teaspoon cornflour

Serves 6

Put lemon rind and juice into a small bowl. Stir in wine or sherry, brandy and sugar until the sugar has dissolved. Cover and leave for several hours to infuse. Strain the liquid into a clean bowl and stir in 300ml (½ pint) of the cream gradually, beating until it almost reaches a soft peak stage (don't use an electric beater. If overbeaten, syllabub will become grainy). Chill overnight.

Next day, top and tail gooseberries and put in a heavy saucepan with the water and 50g (1¾oz) sugar. Simmer gently for about 20 minutes until soft. Rub through a sieve or beat to a pulp. Add 175g (6oz) sugar – you may need more, if gooseberries are tart. Put in a shallow serving bowl and leave to cool.

Bring the remaining 300ml (½ pint) of cream slowly to the boil with strip of lemon rind, and leave on one side to cool a little. Cream egg yolks, cornflour and 25g (1oz) caster sugar together until almost white. Remove lemon rind and pour on the hot cream in a steady stream, beating all the time. Rinse out the saucepan used for heating the cream, leaving a film of water in the bottom. Return egg mixture to pan and heat gently until thick enough to coat the back of a wooden spoon (don't boil because the custard will curdle). Remove from heat and leave to cool. Pour over gooseberry pulp. Sprinkle with caster sugar to stop a skin forming and leave to get completely cold.

Pile prepared syllabub on top of the custard and chill well. Just before serving, decorate with twists of lemon rind or lemon slices and sprigs of fresh rosemary.

Butter'd Oranges

Custard made with butter and eggs was a popular pudding during the 17th and 18th centuries. This recipe is more like an orange cheese or curd rather than a custard. It is very rich but also refreshing.

Thinly pared rind of 2 oranges
Juice of 1 orange
1 tablespoon concentrated orange juice
50g (1¾oz) caster sugar
4 egg yolks
3 egg whites
225g (8oz) unsalted butter
1 large piece candied orange peel
150ml (¼ pint) whipping cream
Slices of fresh orange

Serves 6

Put orange rind in a small saucepan of boiling water and boil for 20 minutes or until soft. Drain and purée rind in a blender or pass through a food mill or just pound orange rind with a rolling pin. Add orange juices and sugar to peel and beat until the sugar has dissolved. Add egg yolks and egg whites and whisk until mixture is thick and smooth. Melt the butter and leave until cool, but not beginning to harden. Pour butter in a steady stream into egg and orange mixture and blend in a liquidizer for about 3 minutes, or beat with a rotary whisk for about 10 minutes. Refrigerate, beating occasionally until thick and beginning to set. Cut candied orange rind into tiny pieces, or shred with a grater. Fold into half-set orange custard. Pour into individual glasses or custard pots and chill well. Decorate, before serving, with whipped cream and orange slices.

Old English Sherry Trifle

FOR THE BASE

1 fatless sponge cake made with 3
    eggs, 85g (3oz) caster sugar and 85g
    (3oz) plain flour or 1 packet of
    trifle sponges

Good-quality apricot jam or apple or
    quince jelly

115g (4oz) ratafia biscuits or
    macaroons

About 6 tablespoons medium sherry
    or Madeira

2 tablespoons brandy (optional)

FOR THE CUSTARD

600ml (1 pint) single or double cream

1 vanilla pod, split in half lengthways

50g (1¾oz) caster sugar

2 teaspoons cornflour

6 egg yolks

FOR THE TOPPING

425ml (¾ pint) double or whipping
    cream

Icing sugar, to sweeten

Serves 6–8

Cut the sponge into 2.5cm (1in) slices and liberally spread with chosen preserve. Arrange in a large glass bowl. Scatter over the ratafia biscuits, then sprinkle liberally with sherry or Madeira and brandy, if using.

To make the custard, bring milk or cream with vanilla pod to the boil. Mix sugar with cornflour, add egg yolks gradually and beat well until smooth. Remove vanilla pod from the milk and pour on to the egg mixture, stirring all the time. Rinse out the milk pan, leaving a film of cold water in the bottom. Return custard to the pan and stir well with a wooden spoon over a low heat until thick. Immediately the custard is thick enough, plunge the bottom of the pan into a bowl of cold water to stop mixture curdling. Leave to cool a little.

When the custard is fairly cool, pour over the sponge, and leave to cool completely. When cool, whip cream until it stands in peaks and spread a thick layer over the custard. Pipe the top with remaining cream and decorate with lots of crystallized fruits, nuts and extra ratafias – the more the merrier, especially at Christmas. In the summer, the trifle looks lovely decorated with crystallized flowers, rose petals or fresh edible flowers.

Trinity Burnt Cream

Also known as Cambridge Cream or Trinity Pudding, this pudding was first introduced to Trinity College, Cambridge by a Fellow in 1879 and served at dinner during May Week. It was brought in on a large silver dish and the caramelized top was cracked with great ceremony.

The recipe is said to have been based on an ancient Scottish dish which may have been brought over from France by Mary, Queen of Scots. It is similar to the delicious French crème brulée. There are endless versions of this creamy pudding with different flavourings – lemon rind, vanilla pod, or a bay leaf. The sugary top used to be browned by a 'salamander', a flat iron which was heated and passed over the top of the pudding.

You can make this custard in one large baking dish or individual ovenproof dishes, and it is best made the day before you want to serve.

600ml (1 pint) double cream
1 vanilla pod split lengthways
5 egg yolks
1 tablespoon caster sugar
About 4 tablespoons demerara sugar

Serves 4–6

Bring the cream with the vanilla pod very gently to the boil, in a saucepan. Leave to cool a little, then remove the vanilla pod. Cream the egg yolks and sugar together in a basin until almost white. Pour the hot cream on to the yolks in a steady stream, whisking all the time. Strain into a shallow 700ml (1¼ pint) ovenproof dish and place in a roasting tin filled with enough hot water to come halfway up the sides of the dish. Cook in a preheated oven at 150°C, 300°F, gas mark 2 for 1–1¼ hours or until just set. Remove the dish from the oven and leave until cold. Chill in the refrigerator overnight, if possible. Just before serving, spread the demerara sugar in an even layer over the surface of the custard and spray with a little water (this helps caramelize). Heat a grill to its highest temperature, then place the pudding as near to the grill as possible until the sugar has melted and caramelized (if you have a chef's blowtorch, use this instead). Return the pudding to the refrigerator for 30 minutes before serving, decorated with a few edible flowers and accompanied by a bowl of fresh cherries, strawberries or raspberries in season.

Rich Cabinet Pudding with Orange Sauce

*Also called Charter Pudding, Chancellor's Pudding, Diplomatic Pudding, Newcastle
Pudding or Ratafia Pudding. It is a rich custard dating back to the 19th century, when it
was thickened with sponge cakes and ratafias and ornamented with glacé cherries and
angelica. Cabinet Pudding is best made in a charlotte tin but a 12.5cm (5in) cake tin or
soufflé dish will do.*

1 tablespoon brandy
1 teaspoon orange rind, grated
1 teaspoon candied orange peel
A little unsalted butter
A few natural glacé cherries, halved
A little crystallized angelica
2 trifle sponges
25g (1oz) ratafia biscuits
600ml (1 pint) single cream
1 vanilla pod, split in half lengthways

6 eggs
1 tablespoon caster sugar
1 teaspoon cornflour

FOR THE ORANGE SAUCE
150ml (¼ pint) fresh orange juice
Caster sugar to taste
A little potato flour or arrowroot
½ teaspoon finely grated orange
   rind

Serves 6

Soak the grated orange rind and candied peel in the brandy. Grease a straight-sided charlotte mould
or soufflé dish with the unsalted butter and line the bottom with buttered greaseproof paper or foil.
Decorate the bottom with a few glacé cherry halves and angelica cut into diamond shapes. Cut the
sponges into small squares and arrange over the candied fruit in the mould, with the ratafias
crumbled into pieces on top.

   Bring the cream and vanilla pod to the boil very slowly, then cool a little. Cream the eggs, sugar
and cornflour together in a basin, then strain the cream on to the egg mixture, stirring vigorously.
Add the soaked orange rind, peel and brandy to the custard, then pour carefully over the cake in the
mould. Leave to soak for about 15 minutes, then cover tightly with foil and tie down with string.
Steam gently for about 1 hour or until the custard is set and firm.

   Meanwhile, make the sauce. Bring the orange juice and sugar to the boil. Mix a little potato flour
or arrowroot in a tablespoon of cold water, stir this into the boiling juice a little at a time until you
have the required consistency. Add the grated orange rind. Dredge with caster sugar to prevent a skin
forming. Serve the pudding hot with a little orange sauce.

Pies, Tarts and Flans

The British have as great a claim as any nation to being experts in the art of pie and tart making. Their recipes for sweet pies and tarts have hardly changed over the centuries since the Middle Ages. The majority of the populace had to take their pies to communal ovens or pie-makers to be baked as the equipment, space, fuel and technology were only available to the relatively well-off.

The pie developed from the Roman idea of sealing meat or fish inside a flour and oil paste to cook it. This paste case or 'coffyn' was not eaten, but discarded or given to the dogs. By medieval times in northern Europe, where butter and lard were the common cooking fats, pastry began to be made that was strong and pliable enough to be moulded into a freestanding container. Thus the 'stand' pie was invented – the ancestor of our modern 'raised' pie.

By the 15th century, pies had become very popular and there was an enormous variety. Most meat and fish pies included dried fruit, spices, apples, gooseberries, sugar and honey so it was not easy to tell a savoury from a sweet pie. By Elizabethan times, shorter richer pastry was being made, sometimes including butter and eggs. Pies became more and more elaborate.

Sweetened meat and dried fruit pies and standing pies began to go out of fashion in the Georgian period. Fruit tarts and pies were becoming much more adventurous and were now prepared in dishes or tins – the 'dish pye'. A large variety of fruits were put into pies, together with luxurious fillings like chocolate, chestnuts and almonds. Many of these recipes have remained more or less in their original form.

Tarts were made of short rich pastry, which became richer and shorter as the centuries progressed. Really rich bitter paste or 'puff paste' was used in Elizabethan times to make fruit tarts and, later, for jam tarts and patties. Some Elizabethan tart fillings or 'tartstuff' might seem strange to modern tastes – prunes, medlars, quinces and rosehips were stewed with sugar, red wine, cinnamon, ginger and rose water. Flowers prepared in the spring and summer were also popular as tart fillings.

There is such an enormous variety of pies, tarts and flans, all interesting historically and good to eat, that I have found it extremely difficult to choose just a few for this book. I have tried to include some of the old favourites as well as mentioning others that might have been long forgotten.

Apple and Cheesecrust Pie

British apples are among the best in the world. Even the most chauvinistic of the world's 'grandes cuisines' are compelled to acknowledge their quality, as well as that of English apple pie, which is at its traditional best served with cream, or good English Cheddar or Wesleydale cheese, must surely rank among the world's top puddings.

Apple pies were flavoured with candied orange peel, saffron, cloves, cinnamon and dates until the 18th century, when lemon rind and juice was favoured and this combination has continued to be popular. Wild fruits like blackberries, bilberries and elderberries were added by the poor, to make the apples and the pie go further.

The traditional combination of apple and cheese has inspired the use of cheese pastry in this recipe.

FOR THE PASTRY
175g (6oz) plain flour
115g (4oz) butter, cut in small pieces
115g (4oz) Cheddar cheese, finely
  grated
1 egg yolk
About 1 tablespoon ice-cold water

FOR THE FILLING
700g (1lb 9oz) Bramley apples
225g (8oz) Cox's apples
50g (1¾oz) butter
About 85g (3oz) soft brown sugar
Pinch of ground cinnamon
Grated rind of ½ lemon
50g (1¾oz) raisins (optional)
Juice of 1 lemon
A little milk and caster sugar, to glaze

Serves 6

To make the cheese pastry, sieve the flour into a mixing bowl, then rub in the butter. Stir in the grated cheese, then mix to a dough with the egg yolk and water. Knead lightly, then chill in the refrigerator.

Cut each apple into thick slices and fry gently in the butter, sprinkling with sugar. Add the cinnamon and lemon rind, then place in a shallow, buttered 23cm (9in) pie dish with the raisins, if using. Pour over the lemon juice and leave to cool.

Roll out the chilled pastry and use to make a lid for the pie. Decorate as you wish, make a hole in the centre, then brush with milk and sprinkle with caster sugar. Bake in a preheated oven at 190°C, 375°F, gas mark 5 for 20–30 minutes, or until the apples are tender and the pastry is golden brown.

Serve warm with Vanilla Custard Sauce (see page 29) or cream.

Taffety Tart

These apple and orange tarts used to be a great favourite in the 18th century. Originally, apple purée was mixed with marmalade and candied orange peel, but here grated apple is combined with orange segments and baked in an orange-flavoured pastry case.

FOR THE PASTRY
175g (6oz) plain flour
50g (1¾oz) semolina
2 tablespoons icing sugar
Pinch of salt
Grated rind and juice of 1 orange
115g (4oz) butter

FOR THE FILLING
1 large orange
2 large eggs
115g (4oz) caster sugar
1 large Bramley apple, peeled and
 grated

Serves 4–6

To make the pastry, sieve the flour, semolina, icing sugar and salt together into a mixing bowl. Gently heat the orange rind, juice and butter in a small pan until bubbling. Remove from the heat and leave to cool for a few minutes. Gradually stir into the flour mixture to make a dough. Roll out and use to line a buttered 20cm (8in) flan tin. Chill well for 30 minutes, then bake blind in the usual way (see Apricot Amber Pudding, page 17).

To make the filling, grate the rind of the orange, then remove the segments taking off the pith and reserving as much juice as possible. Beat the eggs and sugar together well and add the orange segments, rind, juice and grated apple. Pour into the cooled pastry case and bake in a preheated oven at 180°C, 350°F, gas mark 4 for about 30 minutes until the top is golden.

Serve warm with Vanilla Custard or Creamy Marmalade Sauce (see pages 29 and 156), Marmalade Ripple or Vanilla Ice Cream (see page 57 and 59) or with cream. Also very good cold with cream.

Variation

Dorset Apple and Lemon Tart
As before, but use 2 grated apples and the rind and juice of 1 lemon (not the flesh). Reduce the quantity of sugar to 115g (4oz). Serve warm with Vanilla Custard Sauce, Vanilla Ice Cream (see pages 29 and 59) or cream, or cold with cream.

Seville Orange Tart

Oranges began to arrive in England at the end of the 13th century from southern Europe, but were extremely expensive and always of the bitter Seville type. It wasn't until the 16th century that sweet oranges were first brought back from Ceylon by the Portuguese.

Use Seville oranges when in season for this recipe, or sharpen sweet oranges with the juice of a lemon.

175g (6oz) sweet shortcrust pastry (see Chocolate and Prune Tart page 119, but add grated rind of ½ lemon)

FOR THE FILLING
Grated rind and juice of 2 Seville oranges
60g (2oz) caster sugar
60g (2oz) cake crumbs (Madeira-type)
25g (1oz) butter, cut into small pieces
150ml (¼ pint) single cream or full-cream milk
2 eggs, separated

Serves 6

Roll out the pastry and use to line a 23cm (9in) flan ring. Chill, then bake blind (see Apricot Amber Pudding, page 17). Reduce the oven to 180°C, 350°F, gas mark 4.

Mix the orange rind with the sugar until it turns yellowy-orange, then add the cake crumbs and the butter. Warm the cream or milk and pour over the mixture. Stir until the butter has melted, then stir in the egg yolks and the orange juice. Whisk the egg whites until they stand in soft peaks, then fold in gently. Spoon the mixture into the pastry case and bake for 30 minutes until set and golden brown. Serve warm or cold with cream.

Walnut and Honey Tart

Walnuts have been grown in Britain for centuries. Villagers used to gather them in the autumn and make them into pies, puddings, sauces, cakes, soups and stuffings. They were also added to meat and fish dishes and pickled. This traditional tart is very rich, so serve in small portions.

175g (6oz) shortcrust pastry

FOR THE FILLING
85g (3oz) butter
125g (4½oz) soft brown sugar
Grated rind of 1 orange
3 eggs
175g (6oz) clear honey
A few drops of vanilla essence
110g (4oz) broken walnuts
Walnut halves for decorating

Serves 6–8

Roll out the chilled pastry and use to line a 20cm (8in) flan ring. Bake blind in the usual way (see Apricot Amber Pudding, page 17).

Cream the butter, gradually adding the sugar and the orange rind. Beat until well-blended, then beat the eggs and add gradually to the creamed mixture, beating continuously. Add the honey and vanilla essence, mixing to a smooth consistency. Stir in the broken walnuts, then pour into the pastry case. Arrange walnut halves on top, then bake in the centre of a preheated oven at 200°C, 400°F, gas mark 6 for about 40 minutes, or until set. Protect the top with foil if it is browning too quickly.

Remove from the oven and leave to cool, then serve with plenty of chilled cream.

Apple Pasties

A pasty refers to any sweet and savoury ingredients folded and enclosed in pastry. It is the pride of the West Country, especially Cornwall. Originally the pasty was invented for the men to take to work to keep them going through the long working day. This recipe is a very popular pudding at one of my local pubs. Any flavourings and spices can be added, and try using different combinations of fruit – apple and blackberry, apple and raspberry, apricot and gooseberry.

350g (12oz) shortcrust pastry

FOR THE FILLING
3–4 cooking apples
about 115g (4oz) caster or brown sugar
½ level teaspoon ground cinnamon
1 level tablespoon cornflour
2 teaspoons lemon juice
50g (1¾oz) sultanas or raisins
1 small egg
1 tablespoon cold water
Sifted icing sugar, for dredging

Serves 4–6

Peel, core and slice apples and put in a saucepan with the sugar and cinnamon. Combine cornflour and lemon juice together to make a paste and then add to the saucepan. Cook over low heat until apples are tender, but not broken up, stirring frequently. Remove from heat and allow to cool. Add sultanas or raisins and taste for sweetness.

Roll out the pastry on a lightly floured board to about 3mm (⅛in) thickness and cut into 4 circles 20cm (8in) in diameter or 6 smaller circles. Divide the apple mixture between circles, and draw up edges of pastry to make a seam across the top, pinching edges together firmly. Crimp edges together to make a neat ridge. Place on a greased baking tray and chill again.

Beat the egg with 1 tablespoon water. Brush glaze over pasties and make a slit in the top of each one. Bake in a preheated oven at 220°C, 425°F, gas mark 7 for 20–30 minutes or until golden brown.

Serve hot or cold with clotted or whipped cream. Try removing a small piece of pastry from the top of each pasty and putting in a dollop of clotted cream – delicious!

Richmond Maids of Honour

Similar recipes go back to the Middle Ages, but these particular little almond-flavoured curd tarts were great favourites at the court of Henry VIII in Richmond Palace, particularly with Anne Boleyn. Henry is said to have named them after her when he saw her eating them while she was maid of honour to Catherine of Aragon, his first wife. Puff pastry is traditional, but rich shortcrust or rough puff is suitable.

225g (8oz) puff pastry (bought or homemade)
2 tablespoons quince or apple jelly or apricot jam

FOR THE FILLING
225g (8oz) curd or cottage cheese
85g (3oz) caster sugar
Grated rind of 1 lemon
50g (1¾oz) ground almonds
2 eggs
1 tablespoon brandy (optional)
Icing sugar, for dusting

Makes about 18

Grease some patty or tartlet tins. Roll out pastry very thinly and using a 8cm (3¼in) cutter, cut out rounds of pastry to line tins. Spoon a little jelly or jam into the bottom of each pastry case. Chill while you prepare the filling.

Sieve curd or cottage cheese into a bowl and mix in caster sugar, lemon rind and ground almonds. Beat eggs, add brandy if using, and add to curd mixture. Mix very thoroughly until well blended. Fill each pastry case two-thirds full with cheese mixture. Bake in the centre of a preheated oven at 200°C, 400°F, gas mark 6 for about 25 minutes or until well risen and puffy. Serve warm or cold, dusted with sieved icing sugar and with clotted or pouring cream.

Variation

Yorkshire Curd Cheesecake
Make one large tart, instead of individual ones, as before, using rich shortcrust instead of puff pastry. Omit the jelly or jam, but add 1 tablespoon currants or raisins to the cheese mixture, leaving out 25g (1oz) caster sugar. Bake for 30–40 minutes or until filling is golden brown and puffy.

Mucky Mouth Pie

A traditional fruit pie from the north of England made with apples, bilberries and fresh mint. For many centuries the latter was thought to be aphrodisiac, but who knows whether northern housewives were aware of this? Certainly this pie was a favourite with their menfolk.

The pastry lid is 'iced' in the traditional way, so the fruit needs to be on the sharp side. If you don't want to use bilberries, blackcurrants, blackberries, blueberries or damsons are all suitable.

225g (8oz) shortcrust pastry

FOR THE FILLING
2 large Bramley apples
450g (1lb) bilberries
A little caster sugar
2 tablespoons fresh mint, finely chopped

FOR THE ICING
115g (4oz) icing sugar
1 large egg white

Serves 6

Chill the pastry, then roll out half of it and use to line a buttered 20cm (8in) pie plate or flan ring. Prick the base of the pastry, then chill again.

Peel, core and slice the apples and cook them to a purée with a very little water. Mix with the bilberries and chopped mint. Sprinkle with a little sugar – not too much because of the sweet icing on top of the pie. Spoon the fruit mixture into the flan ring or pie plate and roll out the rest of the pastry to make a lid. Bake in a preheated oven at 200°C, 400°F, gas mark 6 for about 25 minutes, then remove from the oven and leave to cool slightly. Reduce the oven to 180°C, 350°F, gas mark 4.

To prepare the icing, whisk the egg white until very stiff, then whisk in the sieved icing sugar until the mixture stands in peaks. Spread thickly over the pie crust and put back in the oven for about 10 minutes, until the icing hardens and is very slightly browned.

Serve warm with cream.

Right: Mucky Mouth Pie

Royal Pye

In Elizabethan times a 'royal pye' was any savoury or sweet pie which was 'iced' with sugar and egg white, more like modern royal icing than meringue, which is a descendant. This particular Royal Pye is filled with mincemeat, apples and grapes and is ideal for serving at Christmas alongside, or instead of, the plum pudding. The rich shortcrust pastry was originally called 'biscuit crust'.

Sweet shortcrust pastry made with 175g (6oz) flour

FOR THE FILLING
450g (1lb) Cox's apples
115g (4oz) seedless green grapes
450g (1lb) homemade or good quality mincemeat
1–2 tablespoons brandy or sherry
2 egg whites
115g (4oz) caster sugar

Serves 6–8

After making your pastry, chill in the refrigerator for 30 minutes, then roll out and use to line a buttered 23cm (9in) flan tin. Chill again for about 15 minutes. Preheat the oven to 200°C, 400°F, gas mark 6 and bake blind in the usual way (see Apricot Amber Pudding, page 17).

Peel, core and chop the apples. Halve the grapes if large. Mix the apples and grapes with the mincemeat, stir in the brandy or sherry, then spoon into the pastry case. Cook in the preheated oven at 190°C, 375°F, gas mark 5 for 30 minutes.

Whisk the egg whites until stiff and whisk in half the caster sugar until smooth and glossy. Gently fold in remaining sugar and pile meringue on top of the pie. Put back in the oven and bake for a further 15–20 minutes until meringue is crisp and lightly brown. Serve warm with cream or a hard sauce (see page 157).

Variation

Almond Royal Pye
Use almond pastry instead of a rich shortcrust – 225g (8oz) plain flour, 115g (4oz) butter, 25g (1oz) caster sugar, 25g (1oz) ground almonds and 3 tablespoons ice-cold water.

Left: Royal Pye

A Blackcurrant and Cinnamon Plate Pie

This pie, baked on a plate, is made with cinnamon-flavoured pastry. Try experimenting with various spices and different fruits.

FOR THE PASTRY
225g (8oz) plain flour
Pinch of salt
1 dessertspoon ground cinnamon
50g (1¾oz) butter or margarine
50g (1¾oz) lard
3 tablespoons cold water

FOR THE FILLING
450g (1lb) fresh or frozen
   blackcurrants
115g (4oz) caster sugar
Knob of softened butter
Milk and caster sugar, for
   glazing

Serves 6

Sieve flour, salt and cinnamon together into a mixing bowl. Rub in fats until mixture resembles breadcrumbs. Add enough water to mix to a firm dough. Knead lightly until smooth, and chill. Put blackcurrants and sugar in a saucepan. Cook over gentle heat until juices begin to run, then cook more rapidly for a few minutes, stirring frequently until the blackcurrants look thick and rich. Taste and add more sugar if necessary. Turn into a dish and cool.

Roll out pastry thinly on a lightly floured board. Using half the pastry, line a buttered 20–23cm (8–9in) ovenproof plate. Prick the bottom of the pastry with a fork, brush with softened butter (this will help to prevent pastry at the bottom from going too soggy) and chill for a few minutes. Fill the plate with cooked blackcurrants. Roll out remaining pastry to make a lid, dampening edges and pressing together well to seal. Flute edges of pie. Cut a 5cm (2in) cross in the centre of the top of the pie and fold back each triangle of pastry to make an open square showing the blackcurrants. Brush pastry with milk and sprinkle with caster sugar. Bake near the top of a preheated oven at 220°C, 425°F, gas mark 7 for 10 minutes to set the pastry and then decrease temperature to 180°C, 350°F, gas mark 4 for a further 20–25 minutes. Serve hot or cold, sprinkled with more caster sugar and with cinnamon-flavoured whipped cream or clotted cream piled on the square of blackcurrants showing on top of the pie.

Variation

Cranberries, raspberries, blackberries, redcurrants and bilberries all make excellent plate pies with the cinnamon pastry.

Orange-flower Cheese Tart

Cheesecakes were originally baked in a pastry case, but I prefer a biscuit crumb base. However, do try both and see which you like. Orange flower water was substituted for rose water in some English dishes towards the end of the 17th century. Few English gardens had fallen orange blossoms to make this scented water, so it was usually imported from France or Portugal. Both orange flower and rose water continued in popularity as food flavourings all through the 18th century, but then lost favour. Recently, there has been a renewed interest and they can be bought at grocers or chemists. Cream cheese has been made in Britain since Roman times and a cheesecake of a similar recipe dates back to the 17th century. It is not, as some people may imagine, a modern invention from North America. Bake this tart the day before serving.

225g (8oz) digestive biscuits
225g (8oz) butter
700g (1lb 9oz) cream cheese
225g (8oz) caster sugar
3 eggs

1 teaspoon orange flower water
1 level tablespoon grated orange rind
150ml (¼ pint) soured cream
Fresh orange slices, for decorating

Serves 12

Put biscuits in a plastic bag and crush with a rolling pin. Melt 115g (4oz) butter and mix together with biscuit crumbs in a mixing bowl. Press into a 23cm (9in) spring-release cake tin to cover base. Refrigerate while making filling.

In a large mixing bowl, beat cream cheese until smooth. Slowly beat in sugar until evenly blended. Add remaining butter, melted in a small saucepan, beaten eggs, orange flower water and grated orange rind. Continue beating until mixture is really smooth. Pour into chilled crumb base. Bake in the centre of a preheated oven at 150°C, 300°F, gas mark 2 for 45 minutes. Turn off oven, but leave cheesecake in the oven for a further 30 minutes. Remove from oven and cool. Leave in a cool place overnight if possible.

To serve, remove sides of tin and loosen cheesecake from the base with a palette knife. Slide it on to a plate and spread the top with soured cream. Decorate with fresh orange twists.

Variation

Fruit-topped Cheesecake
Make cheesecake as before but top with fresh redcurrants, raspberries, strawberries, cranberries, rhubarb, cherries, blackcurrants or blackberries. Glaze if you wish with melted redcurrant or apple jelly.

Cherry and Brandy Dish Pie

Cherry pies and 'bumpers', or pasties, were baked and eaten at cherry pie feasts to celebrate the harvesting of the fruit, in the principal cherry-growing areas of England, such as Kent and Buckinghamshire.

FOR THE PASTRY
225g (8oz) plain flour
Pinch of salt
115g (4oz) butter
25g (1oz) caster sugar
1 egg yolk
About 2 tablespoons ice-cold water

FOR THE FILLING
900g (2lb) stoned cherries
About 115g (4oz) caster sugar
Knob of butter
Milk and caster sugar, for glazing
2 tablespoons cherry brandy or brandy
3 tablespoons double cream

Serves 6

Sieve flour and salt together into a mixing bowl. Rub in butter until mixture resembles breadcrumbs. Stir in caster sugar, egg yolk and enough cold water to mix to a firm dough. Knead lightly until smooth and chill for at least 30 minutes. Fill a 850ml (1½ pint) pie dish with stoned cherries, sprinkle with sugar and dot with butter.

Roll out pastry on a lightly floured board and cover dish of cherries. Flute edges of pastry lid and make a couple of slits in the top to let out the steam. Decorate with pastry trimmings. Brush with milk and caster sugar. Bake in the centre of a preheated oven at 200°C, 400°F, gas mark 6 for 20 minutes, then reduce heat to 180°C, 375°F, gas mark 5 and continue cooking for 20–25 minutes or until pastry is golden brown.

Remove from oven and cut neatly round the lid of the pie. Lift off carefully, and pour cherry brandy or brandy and cream over the fruit. Replace pastry lid, dredge with extra caster sugar and return to the oven for 5 minutes. Serve hot with whipped or clotted cream.

Variation

Summer Fruit and Brandy Pie
Use a combination of soft summer fruits instead of cherries – 450g (1lb) raspberries with 225g (8oz) blackcurrants and 225g (8oz) redcurrants. Use brandy instead of cherry brandy. Serve with whipped or clotted cream.

Quince and Pear Doublecrust Pie

Quinces, pears and apples were once put into pies with wine and spices and baked for four hours. I promise you this recipe is quicker! If you have trouble buying quinces, use extra pears or apples instead.

300g (10½oz) puff pastry
1 egg
1 tablespoon milk

FOR THE FILLING
500ml (18fl oz) water
100g (3½oz) caster sugar
1 vanilla pod, split in half lengthways
3 quinces
Juice of 1 lemon
3 ripe pears
1 tablespoon redcurrant jelly

Serves 8

Bring the water, sugar and vanilla pod to the boil in a pan, then simmer very gently for about 15 minutes. Peel and core the quinces and roll them in lemon juice to prevent browning. Cut into 6mm (⅜in) slices and roll in the lemon juice again. Remove with a slotted spoon and poach in the vanilla sugar syrup for 45 minutes, or until the quinces turn pink and are tender. Allow them to cool in this liquid. Roll the pastry out into 2 circles, 30cm (12in) in diameter and chill for 30 minutes.

Drain the quinces thoroughly in a colander or sieve and then on kitchen paper, reserving their liquor for later. Peel, core and slice the pears the same size as the quinces. Toss them in the leftover lemon juice, then mix the two fruits together well.

Lay one of the pastry discs on a buttered baking tray and pile on the fruit, leaving a border 2.5cm (1in) all around. Beat the egg with the milk and brush the border of pastry with it. Now lay the second disc of pastry over the fruit, pressing the edges of pastry together well. Using the back of a small knife, knock up the edges of the pastry and make a small hole in the top of the pie. Glaze the top with the egg mixture. Bake in a preheated oven at 200°C, 400°F, gas mark 6 for about 35 minutes, or until golden brown (be careful it doesn't burn). Reduce the reserved quince cooking liquor to about 6 tablespoons, then whisk in the redcurrant jelly.

Serve the pie lukewarm with this sauce at the same temperature. Eat with Vanilla Custard Sauce or Vanilla Ice Cream or (see pages 29 and 59) or thick cream.

Cumberland Rum Nicky

Small versions of this pie, similar to mince pies and called Rum Nickies, can also be made. It recalls the days in the 18th century when Whitehaven in Cumbria was one of the leading ports in the rum trade with the West Indies.

FOR THE PASTRY
225g (8oz) plain flour
Pinch of salt
115g (4oz) butter
25g (1oz) caster sugar
1 egg yolk
2–3 tablespoons ice-cold water

FOR THE FILLING
115g (4oz) chopped dates
50g (1¾oz) chopped preserved ginger
50g (1¾oz) butter
25g (1oz) caster sugar
2 tablespoons dark rum
Icing sugar for dredging

Serves 6

Sieve flour and salt together into a mixing bowl. Rub in butter until mixture resembles breadcrumbs. Stir in half the sugar. Add egg yolk and enough ice-cold water to mix to a firm dough. Knead lightly until smooth. Chill for at least 30 minutes.

Roll out pastry on a lightly floured board. Line a greased 20cm (8in) pie or ovenproof plate with half the pastry. Sprinkle over chopped dates and ginger. Cream butter and remaining sugar together until pale and fluffy. Beat in rum gradually. Spread mixture over fruit in pie plate. Cover with remaining pastry, sealing edges well. Make a couple of slits in the top of the pastry, flute edges and decorate as you wish with pastry trimmings. Bake in the centre of a preheated oven at 200°C, 400°F, gas mark 6 for 10–15 minutes and then reduce temperature to 180°C, 350°F, gas mark 4 for a further 25–30 minutes. Serve hot, dredged with icing sugar and with whipped or clotted cream or Rum and Orange Butter (see page 157).

Chocolate and Prune Tart

Chocolate was introduced into Britain in the mid-17th century from Mexico, where the Aztecs had mixed it with honey. It remained a luxury drink as long as the price of sugar was high, and was never as popular as coffee or tea. A pie with a chocolate filling like this would have been considered a great luxury.

FOR THE SWEET SHORTCRUST PASTRY
175g (6oz) plain flour
Pinch of salt
85g (3oz) icing sugar
150g (5½oz) unsalted butter
2 small egg yolks, beaten

FOR THE PRUNE PUREE
300g (10oz) stoned ready-to-eat prunes
2 tablespoons brandy

FOR THE CHOCOLATE FILLING
100g (3½oz) good-quality plain
    chocolate (72% cocoa fat)
2 eggs, separated
300ml (½ pint) double cream
85g (3oz) caster sugar
Sifted icing sugar, to dust

Serves 8–10

To make the pastry, sieve the flour with the salt and icing sugar into a bowl. Rub in the butter, then mix to a soft dough with the egg yolks. Knead very briefly, then wrap in clingfilm and chill in the refrigerator for 30 minutes. Roll out and use to line a buttered, 25cm (10in) flan tin. Bake blind in the usual way (see Apricot Amber Pudding, page 17).

Meanwhile, make the prune purée by simmering the prunes gently with barely enough water to cover, for 5–10 minutes or until very tender. Lift them out with a slotted spoon and process with the brandy and just enough of the juice to make a thick purée (about 3 tablespoonfuls). Spread over the base of the pastry case.

To make the chocolate filling, break the chocolate into pieces and place in a bowl, set over a pan of gently simmering water, making sure that the base of the bowl does not come into contact with the water. Remove the bowl as soon as the chocolate has melted and cool slightly, then beat in the egg yolks one by one. Lightly whip the cream and fold into the chocolate mixture. Whisk the egg whites until they form soft peaks, then sprinkle over the caster sugar and continue to whisk until glossy. Fold into the chocolate mixture, then pour into the pastry case.

Bake in the preheated oven at 200°C, 400°F, gas mark 6, for about 40–50 minutes until puffed, set around the edges, but still wobbly in the centre. Serve warm or cold dusted with icing sugar and with Vanilla Ice Cream, Orange Cream Sauce (see pages 59 and 138), or cream.

Gypsy Tart

An almost forgotten 20th-century classic, this delicious butterscotch tart originated from Kent. If you were at school in the 1950s and 60s you will remember it with affection and it's well worth reviving. Children still love it. I have included nuts in this recipe, to make it more grown-up, but omit them if you want to taste the original.

FOR THE PASTRY
225g (8oz) plain flour
115g (4oz) butter
Cold water to mix

FOR THE FILLING
400g (14 oz) tin evaporated milk, chilled overnight
350g (12 oz) dark muscovado sugar
Chopped walnuts or pecan nuts (optional)
Sifted icing sugar, for dusting

Serves 8

To make the pastry, sieve the flour into a mixing bowl, then rub in the butter until mixture resembles fine breadcrumbs. Add 2–4 tablespoons of cold water and mix to a dough. Knead lightly, then leave to rest for at least 10 minutes in the refrigerator. Preheat the oven to 200°C, 400°F, gas mark 6 with a large baking sheet in the oven to heat up as well.

Roll the pastry out and line a deep, buttered, 25cm (10in) loose-bottomed flan tin. Bake blind in the usual way (see Apricot Amber Pudding, page 17, for instructions).

Meanwhile, whisk the evaporated milk and sugar with an electric whisk, for about 15 minutes. Remove the baking sheet with the pastry case from the oven. Pour the filling into the pastry case and scatter over the chopped nuts if using.

Return to the centre of the oven and bake for a further 10 minutes (the filling will still be slightly wobbly but will set on cooling). Remove from the oven and leave to cool until just warm.

Serve dusted with icing sugar and with pouring cream.

Right: Gypsy Tart
Next page: Chocolate and Prune Tart

Lady's Tart .

This 19th-century tart was originally filled with apricot preserve and decorated with flaked almonds. It had a decorative edge of small pastry circles. In this recipe, I have used four varieties of jam laid in sections and divided by strips of pastry – once the pride of housewives, who, of course, used their best homemade jams.

225g (8oz) shortcrust pastry
2 tablespoons apricot jam
2 tablespoons raspberry or strawberry jam
2 tablespoons blackcurrant jam
2 tablespoons green gooseberry or greengage jam
Milk or water, for brushing
1 egg, beaten
1 tablespoon cold water

Serves 6

Roll out the pastry thinly and use two-thirds of it to line a buttered 25cm (10in) ovenproof plate. Divide the pastry base into 8 sections, marking lightly with a knife. Spread each section with the different jams alternating the colours and avoiding the rim of the plate. Cut the pastry trimmings into narrow strips and arrange in twists across the tart dividing the jams.

Cut the remaining one-third of the pastry into small circles with a 2.5cm (1in) cutter. Brush rim of pastry-lined plate with a little milk or water and arrange the circles around the edge overlapping them a little.

Beat the egg with the water and brush pastry circles and twists carefully to glaze. Bake in the centre of a preheated oven at 190°C, 375°F, gas mark 5 for about 30 minutes or until pastry is golden brown. Serve hot or cold with Vanilla Custard Sauce (see page 29) or with thick cream.

Left: Lady's Tart
Previous page: Lemon Meringue Pie

Lemon Meringue Pie

FOR THE PASTRY
175g (6oz) plain flour
1 tablespoon icing sugar
115g (4oz) cold butter, cut in
    small pieces
1 egg yolk
About 1 tablespoon ice-cold water

FOR THE FILLING
115g (4oz) caster sugar
2 level tablespoons cornflour

Grated rind of 2 large lemons
125ml (4fl oz) lemon juice
Juice of 1 small orange
85g (3oz) butter, cut in small pieces
3 egg yolks
1 whole egg

FOR THE MERINGUE
4 egg whites, at room temperature
225g (8oz) caster sugar
2 level teaspoons cornflour

Serves 6

To make the pastry, sieve the flour and icing sugar together into a mixing bowl. Lightly rub in the butter, then add the egg yolk and enough water to mix to a dough. Knead briefly into a smooth ball, then roll out and line a buttered 23cm (9in) loose-bottomed, fluted flan tin. Prick the base with a fork, line with foil and chill for 30 minutes to 1 hour or overnight. Put a baking sheet in the oven and preheat to 200°C, 400°F, gas mark 6. Bake blind in the usual way (see Apricot Amber Pudding, page 17). Remove from the oven and set aside. Lower the oven to 180°C, 350°F, gas mark 4.

To make the filling, mix the sugar, cornflour and lemon rind in a medium saucepan. Strain and stir in the lemon juice gradually. Make the orange juice up to 200ml (7fl oz) with water and strain into the pan. Cook over a medium heat, stirring continuously, until thick and smooth. Once the mixture bubbles, remove from the heat and beat in the butter until melted. Beat the egg yolks and whole egg together, then add to the pan and return to the heat. Keep stirring vigorously for a few minutes until the mixture thickens and plops from the spoon. Remove from the heat and set aside.

Whisk the egg whites to soft peaks, then add half the sugar, a spoonful at a time, whisking between each addition without overbeating. Whisk in the cornflour, then add the rest of the sugar as before until smooth and glossy. Quickly reheat the filling and pour it into the pastry case. Immediately pile spoonfuls of meringue around the edge of the filling (if you start in the middle, the meringue may sink), then spread so it just touches the pastry (to anchor it and help stop it sliding). Pile the remaining meringue into the centre, spreading so that it touches the surface of the hot filling and starts to cook, then give it all a swirl. Return to the oven for 18–20 minutes until the meringue is crisp.

Remove from the oven and leave in the tin for 30 minutes, then remove and leave for at least another 30 minutes to 1 hour before serving. Eat the same day, or the meringue will be spoiled.

Raspberry and Cream Tart

This delicious tart recipe is based on one which dates back to the 17th century. In the original, the highly spiced raspberries were set in an egg custard and cooked in a thin-lidded puff-pastry pie. Other soft fruits like strawberries, cherries, blueberries and bilberries are successful and almond pastry is delicious, although more difficult to handle.

175g (6oz) sweet shortcrust pastry (see Chocolate and Prune Tart page 119, but add 2–3 drops of vanilla extract to the egg yolks)

FOR THE FILLING
900g (2lb) fresh raspberries
About 115g (4oz) caster sugar
3 large eggs
1 level tablespoon cornflour
300ml (½ pint) single cream
1 tablespoon raspberry liqueur

Serves 6–8

After making and chilling the pastry, use it to line a buttered 25cm (10in) flan tin. Chill again for 15 minutes, then bake blind in the usual way (see Apricot Amber Pudding, page 17). Remove the pastry case from the oven and leave to cool.

Reduce the oven temperature to 180°C, 350°F, gas mark 4. Fill the pastry case with raspberries and sprinkle them with 85g (3oz) caster sugar. Beat the eggs, remaining sugar and cornflour together until almost white. Stir in the cream and liqueur and taste for sweetness. Add more sugar if you wish. Pour the egg mixture over the raspberries and bake in the centre of the oven for 35–40 minutes, or until the custard has just set.

Serve warm with Vanilla Ice Cream (see page 59) or cream.

A Sweet Egg Pie

*Also known as Custard Tart and Transparent Pudding, this pie has been popular since
Elizabethan days when the filling was made with vegetables or fruit, eggs, thick cream and
lots of spices. Originally the pastry case was literally to provide a 'coffyn' or container in
which to cook the custard.*

175g (6oz) sweet shortcrust pastry (see Chocolate and Prune Tart, page 119)

FOR THE FILLING
500ml (18fl oz) whipping cream
1 vanilla pod, split in half lengthways
6 egg yolks
85g (3oz) caster sugar
1 teaspoon cornflour
1 teaspoon rose water (optional)
Freshly grated nutmeg

Serves 4–6

Roll out the pastry and use to line a buttered 20cm (8in), 5cm (2in) deep flan ring. Bake blind in
the usual way (see Apricot Amber Pudding, page 17). Reduce the heat to 150°C, 300°F, gas mark 2.

Meanwhile make the custard filling by pouring the cream into a small pan. Add the vanilla pod and
bring to the boil. Beat the egg yolks, sugar and cornflour together, then pour on the boiling cream. Stir
well, then add the rose water. Pass through a fine sieve, skimming any froth from the surface. Pour the
custard mixture into the baked pastry case, grating plenty of fresh nutmeg across the surface. Place
carefully in the oven and cook for about 30 minutes, or until just set (gently shake the baking tray –
a gentle wobble will indicate that the tart is cooked).

Remove from the oven and allow to cool to room temperature, before serving dusted with icing
sugar. Eat with fresh soft fruit or a sauce, or serve plain (don't put in the refrigerator or the texture
will firm up and spoil).

Rhubarb and Orange Lattice Tart

This traditional tart is made with cinnamon- or ginger-flavoured pastry and filled with rhubarb, flavoured with orange. The lattice top is a traditional way of finishing off a pie – not for decoration but for marking. In the past, the housewife would make a large number of both savoury and sweet pies and bake them all at the same time, either in her own oven or in the village baker's oven, and of course the pies all had to be identified with either lattices, slits, or marks of some description.

FOR THE PASTRY
175g (6oz) plain flour
Pinch of salt
1 teaspoon ground ginger or cinnamon
85g (3oz) butter
25g (1oz) caster sugar
1 egg, beaten
About 2 tablespoons ice-cold water

FOR THE FILLING
450g (1lb) young rhubarb
25g (1oz) plain flour
About 115g (4oz) caster sugar
Grated rind of 1 orange
1 egg, beaten
4 tablespoons orange juice
Milk and caster sugar, for glazing

Serves 6

Sieve the flour, salt and spice into a mixing bowl. Rub in the butter lightly until the mixture resembles breadcrumbs. Stir in the sugar and mix to a firm dough with the beaten egg and water. Roll out thinly and use to line a buttered 20cm (8in) flan tin or pie plate. Chill for 30 minutes, then bake blind in the usual way (see Apricot Amber Pudding, page 17).

Cut the rhubarb into short lengths and arrange in the chilled pastry case. Put the flour, sugar and orange rind in a small basin. Add the beaten egg and blend well until smooth. Heat the orange juice in a small saucepan until it reaches boiling point, then pour on the egg mixture gradually, stirring continuously. Return to the pan and bring to the boil again, stirring all the time. Pour over the rhubarb. Roll the pastry trimmings into long strips 1cm (½in) wide and arrange in a lattice pattern over the top of the tart, twisting them like barley sugar, and sticking the ends down with a little water. Brush each strip with a little milk and sprinkle with sugar.

Bake in a preheated oven at 200°C, 400°F, gas mark 6 for 35–40 minutes, until the rhubarb is tender and the pastry lattice is golden. Serve warm or cold, with Vanilla Custard Sauce (see page 29) or thick cream.

Manchester Tart

Also called Manchester Pudding, as its original form in the 18th century
would have been made in a deep pie dish lined around the side with pastry.

175g (6oz) shortcrust pastry

FOR THE FILLING
300ml (½ pint) full-cream milk
Grated rind of 1 lemon
50g (1¾oz) fresh white breadcrumbs
2 large eggs, separated
50g (1¾oz) butter, melted
1 tablespoon brandy
100g (3½oz) caster sugar
3 tablespoons good-quality jam of your choice

Serves 6

Roll out the pastry and use to line a buttered 20cm (8in) pie plate or shallow flan tin. Bake blind in the usual way (see Apricot Amber Pudding, page 17).

To make the filling, bring the milk to the boil in a pan with the lemon rind. Remove from the heat and allow to cool so that the flavour of the lemon will infuse with the milk. Pour the cooled milk through a sieve over the breadcrumbs. Beat the egg yolks into the mixture, then add the melted butter, brandy and 25g (1oz) of the sugar. Spread your chosen jam into the pastry case and pour over the filling.

Bake in a preheated oven at 180°C, 350°F, gas mark 4 for 40–45 minutes. While the tart is cooking, whisk the egg whites with half the remaining sugar until stiff, then fold in the rest of the sugar. Coat the top of the tart with this meringue, then put back in the oven for about 15 minutes until crisp and lightly browned.

Treacle Tart

With the setting up of sugar refineries in British ports in the late 18th century, treacle, the syrup remaining after the sugar had been refined, was generally available. The origin of treacle tart may be medieval gingerbread, which was made by pressing breadcrumbs, treacle, spices and colourings together. Treacle was later replaced in tarts by golden syrup, but the name remained. In the north it continued to be popular as it was a cheaper sweetener.

175g (6oz) shortcrust, sweet shortcrust or almond pastry

FOR THE FILLING
50g (1¾oz) fresh white breadcrumbs
grated rind and juice of 1 lemon
½ teaspoon ground ginger
6 tablespoons golden syrup
3 tablespoons double cream

Serves 6

Chill the pastry, then roll out thinly and use to line a buttered 20cm (8in) shallow loose-bottomed flan tin. Prick all over and chill for at about 30 minutes, then bake blind in the usual way (see Apricot Amber Pudding, page 17). Remove from the oven and cool briefly.

Mix the filling ingredients together and pour into the pastry case. Bake in a preheated oven at 200°C, 400°F, gas mark 6 for 5 minutes, then reduce to 170°C, 325°F, gas mark 3. Bake for a further 25 minutes, or until golden brown and set.

Remove from the oven and leave to cool for at least 30 minutes, then serve warm with Vanilla Custard Sauce, Honey and Brandy Ice Cream, Vanilla Ice Cream (see pages 29, 55 and 59), or cream.

Steamed and Boiled Puddings

The ancestor of the boiled pudding was the medieval 'pottage', a kind of porridge of cereal, honey, wild fruits and shredded meat or fish. Later, in Tudor and Stuart times, meatless puddings of breadcrumbs, rice or oatmeal were mixed with milk, cream, eggs, spices and dried fruit, stuffed into animal guts and boiled. They were then removed from the guts and browned in front of the fire, and served sprinkled with sugar and melted butter. Although animal guts were useful as containers for boiling puddings, they had several disadvantages, because they were awkward to clean, inconvenient to fill and of course were only available at pig- or sheep-killing time. Experiments were made using other containers such as hollowed turnips, carrots and cucumbers. This practice continued all through the 17th century, but did not lead to any real development in pudding-making.

The future of the boiled suet pudding as one of England's national dishes was assured only when the pudding cloth came into use. It received one of its earliest mentions in a recipe for College Pudding or Cambridge Pudding dated 1617. The invention of the pudding cloth or bag firmly cut the link between puddings and animal guts. Puddings could now be made at any time and they became a regular part of the daily fare of almost all classes. One of the advantages of a pudding wrapped in its pudding cloth was that it could be simmered along with the meat by the poorer housewife, whose principal means of cooking in the 17th century was still a cauldron suspended from a pot-hook over the fire.

Suet was sometimes replaced by bone marrow in boiled puddings. Ground almonds were often an ingredient and dried fruit was added liberally in some recipes to make a 'plum' pudding. It was found that dried fruit did not lose its flavour and consistency as much as fresh fruit, although before the end of the 17th century the boiled pudding, composed of a suet crust wrapped around a filling of apples or gooseberries, had come into existence. Mace, nutmeg, cinnamon and ginger were spices commonly used for seasoning. Heavy suet boiled puddings reached their peak of popularity in Victorian times, when they were much loved by Prince Albert. He was responsible for introducing the 'plum pudding' as part of traditional Christmas fare.

Bachelor's Pudding

2 tablespoons golden syrup
115g (4oz) unsalted butter
115g (4oz) caster sugar
2 eggs
140g (5oz) self-raising flour
2 tablespoons milk or water
450g (1lb) cooking apples
50g (1¾oz) currants
85g (3oz) demerara sugar
1 level teaspoon ground cinnamon

Serves 6

Butter thoroughly a 1.2 litre (2 pint) pudding basin. Pour golden syrup into the bottom. Cream butter and caster sugar together until pale and fluffy. Beat eggs and add gradually to creamed mixture. Fold in flour gently with a metal spoon. Add sufficient milk or water to make a soft dropping consistency. Peel, core and slice apples and mix with currants, demerara sugar and cinnamon. Pour a layer of pudding mixture into the bottom of the prepared basin, top with a layer of apple mixture and then another layer of pudding mixture and then remaining apples. Spoon over remaining pudding mixture. Cover securely and steam for 2–2½ hours until firm and well risen. Turn out on to a warm serving dish and serve with clotted cream or Vanilla Custard Sauce (see page 29).

Brigade Pudding

This is a pudding popular in the north of England, consisting of layers of suet pastry with mincemeat between each layer.

225g (8oz) self-raising flour
Generous pinch of salt
115g (4oz) suet
Grated rind of ½ lemon
6–8 tablespoons cold water
2 tablespoons golden syrup
225g (8oz) mincemeat

Serves 6

Butter a 1.2 litre (2 pint) pudding basin well. Sieve flour and salt together into a mixing bowl, and stir in suet and lemon rind. Add sufficient water to mix to a soft but not sticky dough. Turn on to a floured board and divide into 4 portions, each a little larger than the next. Spoon golden syrup into the bottom of prepared basin. Pat smallest portion of dough into a circle large enough to fit bottom of basin. Spread over a layer of mincemeat, then make another circle of dough to fit the basin. Continue in layers, ending with a top layer of dough. Cover securely and steam for 2½–3 hours. Turn out on to a warm serving plate and serve very hot with Vanilla Custard or Lemon Sauce (see pages 29 and 133).

Variation

De La Ware Pudding
Mix the mincemeat with 2 large cooking apples, cored, peeled and sliced.

College Pudding

Reputed to have been the first pudding boiled in a cloth, it was served to students in the college halls of Oxford and Cambridge as early as 1617.

85g (3oz) self-raising flour
I teaspoon mixed spice
Pinch of salt
85g (3oz) fresh white or brown breadcrumbs
85g (3oz) shredded suet
85g (3oz) raisins
50g (1¾oz) currants
25g (1oz) chopped candied peel
50g (1¾oz) brown sugar
1 egg beaten
About 6 tablespoons milk

Serves 6

Well butter a 1.2 litre (2 pint) pudding basin. Sieve the flour, spice and salt together, then mix with all the dry ingredients in a mixing bowl. Add the beaten egg and enough milk to produce a soft dropping consistency. Spoon into prepared basin, cover securely and steam for 2½ hours.

Turn out on to a warm plate and serve with Vanilla Custard, Lemon or a Hard Sauce (see pages 29, 133 and 157). As children we loved this pudding with a sprinkling of demerara sugar and a large lump of salted butter!

The Duchess's Pudding

A light steamed almond-flavoured sponge pudding with chopped nuts, peel and dried fruit. I don't know which duchess inspired this pudding, but it is delicious and would make a lighter alternative to Christmas pudding.

115g (4oz) unsalted butter
115g (4oz) caster sugar
2 eggs
140g (5oz) self-raising flour
25g (1oz) raisins
25g (1oz) chopped glacé cherries
25g (1oz) chopped candied peel
25g (1oz) chopped walnuts or almonds
A few drops of almond essence
About 2 tablespoons water or milk

Serves 6

Butter a 850ml (1½ pint) pudding basin. Cream butter and sugar together until pale and fluffy. Beat eggs and add gradually to creamed mixture, beating well between each addition. Sieve flour and fold gently into mixture using a metal spoon. Add fruit, peel and nuts, almond essence and enough water or milk to give a soft dropping consistency. Put into prepared basin, cover securely and steam for 1½–2 hours until firm and well risen. When cooked, turn pudding on to a warm serving plate and serve hot with Vanilla Custard, Jam or Lemon Sauce (see pages 29, 92 and below).

Lemon or Orange Sauce

4 tablespoons homemade lemon or orange curd
150ml (¼ pint) single cream

Mix lemon or orange curd and cream together. Heat in a saucepan over a low heat until hot but not boiling. Serve in a warmed jug.

Rich Fig and Almond Pudding

Figs are often associated with religious festivals, and fig pudding was traditionally eaten on Mothering Sunday in Lancashire. Further south in Buckinghamshire and the home counties, figs were eaten on Palm Sunday. This custom was said to be connected with the gospel account of the barren fig tree. The use of figs makes this a very substantial pudding for Christmas.

225g (8oz) dried figs

225g (8oz) stoned dates

115g (4oz) raisins

2 tablespoons brandy, rum or Madeira

225g (8oz) self-raising flour

Pinch of salt

175g (6oz) fresh white breadcrumbs

175g (6oz) suet

50g (1¾oz) ground almonds

3 eggs

Grated rind and juice of 1 lemon

A little milk or water

Serves 6

Chop figs and dates, mix with raisins and sprinkle with brandy, rum or Madeira. Cover and leave to soak for at least 1 hour. Butter a 1.2 litre (2 pint) pudding basin well. Sieve flour and salt together into a mixing bowl. Stir in crumbs, suet and ground almonds. Beat eggs and mix into dry ingredients with lemon rind and juice. Add fruit and mix thoroughly, adding a little milk or water if necessary, to make a soft dropping consistency. Turn into prepared basin, cover securely and steam for 4 hours until firm and well risen. Serve hot with Vanilla Custard or a hard sauce (see pages 29 and 157) or with Madeira Sauce (see below) or clotted cream.

Eliza Acton's Madeira Sauce

Finely pared rind of ¼ lemon

150ml (¼ pint) water

50g (1¾oz) soft brown sugar

25g (1oz) butter

2 level teaspoons cornflour

150ml (¼ pint) Madeira or sweet sherry

Simmer lemon rind, water and sugar in a saucepan for 10–15 minutes. Strain to remove lemon rind. Return syrup to saucepan. Work butter and cornflour together in a small basin. Add small pieces of this creamed mixture to hot syrup to thicken. Add Madeira or sherry, and reheat, but don't boil. Serve hot in a warmed sauceboat.

Apple Hat

A favourite Victorian suet crust pudding filled with juicy apples, raisins and spices. Other seasonal fruits are just as successful – try pears, plums, damsons, greengages, rhubarb or gooseberries. The dried fruit can be omitted, chopped nuts added and alternative spices used.

225g (8oz) self raising flour
Pinch of salt
115g (4oz) suet
6–8 tablespoons cold water
675g (1½lb) cooking apples
50g (1¾oz) raisins or sultanas
85g (3oz) brown or white sugar

3 cloves
Pinch of ground cinnamon
Pinch of ground ginger
Grated rind and juice of ½ lemon
    or 1 orange
50g (1¾oz) unsalted butter
1 tablespoon clotted cream

Serves 6

Sieve flour with salt into a mixing bowl. Stir in suet and mix with sufficient cold water to make a soft, light dough. Knead lightly and roll out on a floured board about 6mm (¼in) thick. Use two-thirds of the pastry to line a prepared basin.

Peel, core and slice apples and fill lined basin with layers of apples, raisins or sultanas, sugar and spices. Add lemon or orange rind and juice and the butter, cut into small pieces. Cover basin with reserved piece of pastry, dampening edges and pressing together firmly. Cover securely and steam for 2–2½ hours.

Turn out on to a warm serving plate and remove a square of the pastry from the top of the pudding. Pop in a tablespoon of clotted cream which will melt into the pudding. Serve hot with Vanilla Custard Sauce (see page 29).

Variations

Apple and Bramble Hat
Use 450g (1lb) cooking apples and 225g (8oz) blackberries. Omit raisins.

Apple and Marmalade Hat
Replace grated rind and juice of lemon with 1–2 tablespoons orange or quince marmalade, and omit raisins. Serve with Marmalade Sauce (see page 155).

Rich Chocolate Pudding

85g (3oz) good-quality plain chocolate
50g (1¾oz) butter
300ml (½ pint) full-cream milk
50g (1¾oz) caster sugar
2 eggs, separated
½ teaspoon vanilla essence
150g (5½oz) fresh white breadcrumbs

Serves 6

Butter a 850ml (1½ pint) pudding basin well. Melt chocolate and butter in a basin over a saucepan of hot water (don't be tempted to use cooking chocolate for this pudding – the flavour will not be as good). Remove chocolate from heat and stir. Warm milk in a saucepan and add gradually to chocolate mixture. Stir in the sugar. Beat egg yolks and add vanilla essence. Stir into chocolate mixture. Add breadcrumbs. Whisk egg whites until stiff and fold gently into pudding mixture. Turn into prepared basin and cover securely. Steam 1½–2 hours until well risen and springy. Serve hot with Easy Chocolate, Chocolate Orange or Chocolate and Coffee Sauce (see pages 56, 154 and 155) or cold with whipped cream.

Variations

Rich Chocolate and Walnut Pudding
Add 85g (3oz) finely chopped walnuts.

Rich Chocolate and Orange Pudding
Add grated rind of 1 orange and ½ lemon and 1 tablespoon brandy.

Right: Rich Chocolate Pudding
Next page: Apple Hat

Spotted Dick

Setting aside the double entendre, the contentious word is thought to be a Huddersfield term for pudding. A Spotted Dick is traditionally made with currants only, but use raisins or a mixture of dried fruits if you wish.

225g (8oz) self-raising flour
Pinch of salt
115g (4oz) suet, butter or margarine
25g (1oz) caster sugar
175g (6oz) currants, soaked in brandy
About 150ml (¼ pint) full-cream milk

Serves 6

Butter a 1.2 litre (2 pint) pudding basin. Sieve together the flour and salt into the basin, then stir in the suet, or rub in the butter or margarine. Add sugar and soaked currants. Mix with enough milk to make a soft dropping consistency. Turn into the basin and cover securely. Steam for 2 hours, then serve very hot with Vanilla Custard, Lemon or Syrup Sauce (see pages 29, 133 and 156).

Variation

Ginger Spotted Dick
Sieve ½ teaspoon ground ginger with flour and salt and add 2 pieces of finely chopped preserved ginger to the currants.

Left: Spotted Dick
Previous page: Orange and Treacle Sponge Pudding

Orange and Treacle Sponge Pudding

FOR THE SAUCE
3 tablespoons golden syrup
Grated rind and juice of 2 oranges
2 tablespoons fresh white breadcrumbs

FOR THE SPONGE
115g (4oz) unsalted butter
115g (4oz) caster sugar
2 eggs
115g (4oz) self-raising flour
About 1 tablespoon cold water

Serves 6

Butter a 850ml (1½ pint) pudding basin thoroughly. Put golden syrup, rind of 1 orange, and juice of 2 oranges into a small heavy saucepan. Warm gently to make a runny sauce. Fold in breadcrumbs and pour sauce into the bottom of prepared basin.

Cream butter and sugar together until pale and fluffy. Beat eggs and add a little at a time to creamed mixture. Sieve flour and gently fold into mixture using a metal spoon. Stir in rind of second orange and enough water to make a soft dropping consistency. Pour the mixture into the prepared basin and cover securely. Steam for 1½–2 hours until well-risen and firm.

Turn out on to a large warm serving plate allowing room for the sauce. Serve with Orange Cream Sauce (see below), Vanilla Custard Sauce (see page 29) or cream.

Orange Cream Sauce

600ml (1 pint) double cream
1 tablespoon caster sugar
Grated rind and juice of 2 oranges

Simmer the cream and sugar together in a large saucepan for about 45 minutes, or until it has reduced by half. Stir in the orange rind and juice and serve.

Golden Syrup Sponge

Still everybody's favourite, this lovely pudding was made across the UK, after golden syrup was first produced in the 19th century.

115g (4oz) butter
115g (4oz) caster sugar
2 eggs
115g (4oz) self-raising flour
Pinch of salt
1–2 tablespoons cold water
3 tablespoons golden syrup

Serves 6

Butter an 850ml (1½ pint) pudding basin thoroughly. Cream butter and sugar together until pale and fluffy. Beat eggs and add a little at a time to creamed mixture, beating well between each addition. Sieve flour and salt together and carefully fold into mixture using a metal spoon. Add enough water to make a soft dropping consistency.

Spoon golden syrup into the buttered basin, then pour on the sponge mixture. Cover securely, then steam for 1½–2 hours until well risen and spongy.

Serve hot with Vanilla Custard, Lemon or Syrup Sauce (see pages 29, 133 and 156), or with clotted cream – particularly good for a summer dinner party in the garden.

Variations

Marmalade or Jam Sponge
Replace golden syrup with good quality marmalade or jam. Serve with Jam or Marmalade Sauce (see pages 92 and 155).

Ginger Syrup Sponge
Sieve 1½ teaspoons ground ginger with the flour.

My Mother's Ginger Pud

I remember this lovely suety pudding from my childhood. My mother adapted a recipe dated 1905 and came up with this 'rib-sticker'. If you are very fond of ginger, try adding a little chopped stem ginger to the mixture before cooking.

115g (4oz) self-raising flour
Pinch of salt
2 heaped teaspoons ground ginger
115g (4oz) fresh white breadcrumbs
115g (4oz) suet
2 heaped tablespoons golden syrup
1 level teaspoon bicarbonate of soda
3 tablespoons milk

Serves 6

Sieve flour, salt and ginger together into a mixing bowl. Stir in breadcrumbs and suet. Melt syrup over a gentle heat until just runny. Dissolve bicarbonate of soda in milk and add to syrup. Pour into dry ingredients and mix well. Turn into a greased 850ml (1½ pint) pudding basin. Cover securely and steam for 2–2½ hours until firm and well risen. Serve hot with Ginger Sauce (see below), Vanilla Custard or Syrup Sauce (see pages 29 and 156), whipped or clotted cream.

Ginger Sauce

2 pieces preserved stem ginger
1 tablespoon caster sugar
1 tablespoon dark rum
150ml (¼ pint) double cream

Chop ginger very finely. Mix with sugar and rum. Stir in double cream and continue stirring until thick. Chill before serving.

Sussex Pond Pudding

175g (6oz) self-raising flour
Pinch of salt
1 level teaspoon baking powder
50g (1¾oz) fresh white breadcrumbs
115g (4oz) suet
150ml (¼ pint) or a little more mixed cold milk and water
175g (6oz) butter
175g (6oz) demerara sugar
1 large thin-skinned lemon

Serves 6

Sift the flour, salt and baking powder into a mixing bowl. Stir in the breadcrumbs and suet. With a round-bladed knife mix in milk and water until you have a soft elastic dough. Form the dough into a ball on a floured board. Generously butter a 1.2 litre (2 pint) pudding basin. Cut off a quarter of the dough and set aside for the lid. Roll out the large piece of dough into a circle about 5cm (2in) wider than the top of the pudding basin and line the basin with this pastry, pressing it to shape.
Cut the butter into rough pieces and put half of it with half the sugar into the pastry-lined basin. Prick the lemon deeply all over with a skewer and lay it on the butter and sugar. Then put the remaining butter and sugar on top. If the mixture is far below the top of the basin you can add some more butter and sugar. Fold the ends of the pastry in over the filling and moisten. Roll out the remaining pastry into a circle to form the lid and lay it on top, pressing the edge to seal. Cover securely and steam for 3½–4 hours, topping up with boiling water if necessary. Turn the pudding out on to a serving dish large enough for the juices to seep out round it. Serve hot with Vanilla Custard Sauce (see page 29) or cream.

Variation

Kentish Well Pudding
Pack 115g (4oz) currants around the lemon and continue as before.

Traditional Christmas Plum Pudding

This did not become associated with Christmas fare until the 19th century, when Prince Albert introduced it because he was so fond of this heavy rich pudding.

Plum porridge or pottage was the earliest form of plum pudding and dates back to medieval times. This was made from meat, usually shin of beef and veal, stewed together with currants, raisins, prunes (the dried plums which give their names to the mixture), spices, sugar, sack, lemon juice and claret. The whole thing was thickened with brown breadcrumbs or sago. By the 19th century, meat had been left out and the pudding became more like our modern-day Christmas pudding.

The idea of putting silver trinkets and charms into the pudding probably came from the earlier tradition of the beans inside the Twelfth Night Cake, but this has since died out. It is still traditional to bury a silver coin, if you have one, in the mixture. All the family should stir the pudding in turn on Stir-up Sunday, the Sunday before Advent, and make a wish at the same time. The coin should then be pushed in, plus a ring and a thimble; the coin is to bring worldly fortune, the ring a marriage and the thimble a life of blessedness.

225g (8oz) large prunes
300ml (½ pint) cold tea
225g (8oz) currants
225g (8oz) sultanas
225g (8oz) large raisins
225g (8oz) self-raising flour
¼ teaspoon salt
½ teaspoon baking powder
1 teaspoon mixed spice
½ teaspoon grated nutmeg
½ teaspoon cinnamon
½ teaspoon ground ginger
450g (1lb) fresh white breadcrumbs
225g (8oz) soft dark brown sugar

225g (8oz) shredded suet
50g (1¾oz) candied citron peel, chopped
50g (1¾oz) candied orange and lemon peel, finely chopped
115g (4oz) blanched almonds, chopped
Grated rind and juice of 1 orange
Grated rind and juice of 1 lemon
115g (4oz) carrot, grated
115g (4oz) cooking apple, grated
300ml (½ pint) stout
3 eggs, beaten
Rum to mix, about 4 tablespoons

Makes 5 x 450g (1lb) puddings

Soak prunes overnight in cold tea. Next day, drain, remove stones and chop finely. The addition of prunes gives a richer, darker colour to the pudding as well as a very good flavour. Wash and dry all remaining dried fruit and stone raisins if necessary.

Sieve flour, salt, baking powder and spices together into a very large bowl. Add breadcrumbs, sugar and suet, mixing in each ingredient thoroughly. Gradually mix in all the dried fruit, candied peel and almonds. Stir in the rind and juice of the lemon and orange, followed by grated carrot and apple. Pour in the stout and mix until smooth. Cover basin with a clean cloth and leave in a cool place overnight or longer if convenient (the flavour will improve). In fact, the mixture can be left to stand for a fortnight or longer at this point. Stir mixture every day if you decide to do this.

On the day you want to cook the puddings, add the beaten eggs. Stir furiously until the pudding ingredients are thoroughly blended. Add enough rum to make a soft dropping consistency. Spoon mixture into greased pudding basins to come within 2.5cm (1in) of rim, packing mixture down well with the back of a wooden spoon. You will need 5 x 450g (1lb) basins or 2 x 900g (2lb) and 1 x 450g (1lb) basins. Cover the top of each with greased greaseproof paper. Put a thick layer of flour on top of the greaseproof paper, pressing it down well (this will become a solid paste and act as a seal both for cooking and storing). Then cover with another piece of greaseproof paper. Finally, cover basins with a pudding cloth, muslin or aluminium foil, making a pleat in the centre to allow room for puddings to rise during cooking. Tie securely with string and make a handle of string across the top of each basin, so that you can lift the puddings in and out of the pan easily.

Place puddings in a steamer, double boiler, or in a large pan of gently boiling water. Steam for at least 6 hours, topping up water level from time to time with boiling water. When cooked, remove puddings from pan and leave until cold. Renew top piece of greaseproof paper and cloth and store in a cool dry place until needed.

On the great day, steam again for 2–3 hours before serving. Turn out on to a large platter. Sprinkle with icing sugar. Heat some brandy, whisky, rum or Kirsch in a small saucepan or ladle. Pour over pudding and set alight. Bring the pudding to the table, burning, and surrounded by a hedge of holly. Any spirit can be used, but you will find that rum burns longer. Make sure your holly doesn't go up in smoke!

Granny's Leg

Also called Spotted Dog, this is a suet roly-poly pudding studded with currants – everybody's idea of a nursery treat. Until the end of the 19th century, it appeared as the first course of a meal to take the edge off the appetite, in the same way as Yorkshire Pudding and any left over was served with the vegetables and meat to make them go further.

175g (6oz) self-raising flour
Pinch of salt
85g (3oz) suet
50g (1¾oz) caster sugar
175g (6oz) currants
4–6 tablespoons milk

Serves 6

Sieve flour and salt together into a mixing bowl. Stir in suet, sugar and currants. Mix in sufficient milk to make a soft dough. Roll out on a floured board to an oblong shape about 20cm (8in) x 30cm (12in) and roll up like a Swiss roll. Wrap loosely in buttered and pleated greaseproof paper and then in pleated kitchen foil so that the pudding has room to expand to keep it light. Steam for 1½–2 hours in a large pan or fish kettle.

When cooked, unwrap pudding, turn out on to a hot dish and serve very hot with Vanilla Custard Sauce (see page 29) or brown sugar and melted butter.

Variations

Mincemeat or golden syrup can be used instead of jam.

Shirt Sleeve Pudding or Suety Jack

Make the dough as before omitting the currants. Roll out as before, then spread thickly with 175–225g (6–8oz) blackcurrant jam, leaving a 2.5cm (1in) border all the way round the edges. Brush these edges with milk and roll up evenly. Pinch the ends well to seal and keep in the jam. Cook as before and serve with Vanilla Custard Sauce (see page 29).

Guard's Pudding

Originally known as Burbridge Pudding and said to be a favourite of the guards, hence its new name. It is a very traditional British steamed pudding, made with raspberry jam.

3 tablespoons good-quality raspberry jam
115g (4oz) butter
115g (4oz) soft brown sugar
115g (4oz) fresh brown breadcrumbs
2 eggs, beaten
Pinch of salt
Grated rind and juice of 1 lemon
1 level teaspoon bicarbonate of soda

Serves 6

Butter a 1.2 litre (2 pint) pudding basin and put a large tablespoon of the jam in the bottom. Cream the butter and sugar together until fluffy, then blend in the remaining jam. Add the breadcrumbs, beaten eggs, salt and lemon rind. Dissolve the bicarbonate of soda in the lemon juice, then add to the mixture. Mix well and turn into the basin. Cover securely, then steam for 2½ hours until well-risen and firm. Serve hot with Vanilla Custard Sauce (see page 29) or cream and Raspberry Sauce (see below).

Raspberry Sauce

225g (8oz) fresh raspberries
85g (3oz) caster sugar
Juice of 1 lemon
2 tablespoons water

Heat all ingredients in a saucepan over a very low heat. Simmer gently for 5 minutes. Rub through a sieve. Taste for sweetness.

Steamed Lemon Curd Pudding

Citrus fruits began to arrive in Britain in the 13th century from the Mediterranean – lemons, oranges, which were of the bitter Seville type, and a few pomegranates. By the end of the Tudor period, lemons were being imported in large quantities and used in perfumes as well as for flavouring food. They have continued in popularity over the centuries. This pudding is very light and a refreshing end to a rich meal.

1 slice lemon
1 rounded tablespoon homemade or good-quality purchased lemon curd
115g (4oz) unsalted butter
115g (4oz) caster sugar
2 large eggs
Grated rind of 2 lemons
140g (5oz) self-raising flour
Pinch of salt
1 level teaspoon baking powder
3 tablespoons lemon juice

Serves 6

Butter a 1.2 litre (2 pint) pudding basin thoroughly. Place slice of lemon in the bottom of the basin and cover it with lemon curd. Cream butter and sugar together until pale and fluffy. Beat eggs then beat into mixture a little at a time. Add lemon rind. Sieve flour, salt and baking powder together and gradually fold into creamed mixture. Mix to a soft dropping consistency with the lemon juice. Spoon mixture into prepared basin. Cover with a piece of buttered foil making a pleat across the top of the basin. Cover securely, then steam for 1½–2 hours until well-risen and firm.

Turn out pudding on to a hot plate – don't leave the lovely lemony topping behind in the basin! Serve hot with Vanilla Custard or Lemon Sauce (see pages 29 and 133).

Variation

Steamed Orange Curd Pudding
Use sweet or Seville oranges and orange curd instead of lemons.

Steamed Lemon and Vanilla Syrup Sponge

FOR THE SYRUP
Grated rind and juice of 2 thin-skinned lemons
200g (7oz) caster sugar
150ml (¼ pint) water
1 vanilla pod

FOR THE SPONGE
175g (6oz) unsalted butter
150g (5½oz) caster sugar
1 thin-skinned lemon
3 eggs, beaten
200g (7oz) plain flour
1½ level teaspoons baking powder
3–4 tablespoons full-cream milk

Serves 6

To make the syrup, pour the lemon juice into a small saucepan with the lemon rind, caster sugar and water. Split the vanilla pod in half lengthways and scrape out the seeds, reserving them for later use. Add the pod to the saucepan and bring to the boil. Simmer until a syrupy consistency is achieved, then reserve.

For the sponge, cream together the butter and sugar with the rind from the lemon and the reserved vanilla seeds until light and fluffy. Gradually add the beaten eggs, then sieve in the flour and baking powder. Add enough milk to make a soft dropping consistency.

Butter a 1.2 litre (2 pint) pudding basin. Cut the zested lemon in half and trim off the top or bottom. Place one of the halves in the bottom of the basin, widest end downwards. Use the other half as you wish. Pour over the reserved syrup, saving a little for later. Carefully spoon the sponge batter into the basin, then cover securely. Steam for about 2 hours, until well-risen and firm.

Turn out on to a warm serving plate and pour over the remaining syrup. Serve with chilled double cream.

Snowdon Pudding

This pudding was re-named after Prince Albert when he came over to England, but this caused a controversy, endangering the peace between England and Wales. It was said very unkindly that 'a bad Albert Pudding will make a good Snowdon Pudding'. However, the original pudding named after the Welsh mountain is much older and brought fame to the hotel at the foot of Snowdon where it was served to hungry climbers and walkers. This is a sponge pudding with sultanas or raisins and lemon rind, originally steamed in a fancy mould lined with orange and lemon shapes and angelica and served with a wine sauce.

115g (4oz) raisins or sultanas
25g (1oz) chopped angelica
115g (4oz) fresh white breadcrumbs
25g (1oz) ground rice or rice flour
115g (4oz) suet
Pinch of salt
25g (1oz) brown sugar
Grated rind of 1 lemon
85g (3oz) lemon marmalade
2 eggs
3–4 tablespoons full-cream milk

Serves 6

Butter a 1.25 litre (2 pint) pudding basin thoroughly. Sprinkle 1 tablespoon raisins or sultanas and chopped angelica over the bottom of buttered basin. Mix together the remaining raisins or sultanas with dry ingredients and lemon rind. Stir in marmalade. Beat eggs and add to mixture with enough milk to make a soft dropping consistency. Spoon carefully into prepared basin. Cover securely, then steam for about 2 hours until well-risen.

Allow to shrink slightly before unmoulding on to a warm serving plate. Serve hot with Eliza Acton's Madeira or Lemon Sauce (see pages 133 and 134).

Canary Pudding

This is one of the basic British light steamed puddings. In the past it would have been made of suet and boiled for at least three hours. Later, it was adapted and given a spongy texture which is much lighter and easier on the stomach. It can be cooked in individual small moulds or darioles and called Castle Puddings or Sutherland Puddings. It was called Canary Pudding, because originally it was made with a flavouring of Madeira, the sweet sherry-like fortified wine from the Canary Islands. Experiment with different flavourings – coffee, lemon, orange and vanilla.

115g (4oz) unsalted butter
115g (4oz) caster sugar
2 eggs
50g (1¾oz) self-raising flour
50g (1¾oz) fresh white breadcrumbs
Grated rind and juice of 1 lemon
1–2 tablespoons Madeira or sweet sherry

Serves 6

Butter a 1.2 litre (2 pint) pudding basin thoroughly. Cream butter and sugar together until pale and fluffy. Beat eggs and add gradually to creamed mixture, beating well between each addition. Sieve flour and gently fold into pudding mixture. Carefully stir in breadcrumbs and lemon rind and mix to a soft dropping consistency with the lemon juice and Madeira or sherry. Spoon into prepared basin, cover securely and steam for about 2–2½ hours or until well risen and spongy. Serve hot with Vanilla Custard Sauce, Lemon Sauce or Eliza Acton's Madeira Sauce (see pages 29, 133 and 134).

Variation

Black Cap Canary Pudding
Put 3 tablespoons blackcurrant jam in the bottom of the basin before filling with pudding mixture.

Date and Walnut Pudding

A very popular pudding from the early 19th century.

115g (4oz) roughly chopped dates
1 tablespoon rum
85g (3oz) self-raising flour
Pinch of salt
½ teaspoon mixed spice
85g (3oz) fresh white or brown breadcrumbs
85g (3oz) suet
2 heaped tablespoons soft brown sugar
50g (1¾oz) roughly chopped walnuts
2 eggs
1–2 tablespoons milk or water

Serves 6

Soak chopped dates in the rum while you prepare pudding. Butter thoroughly a 850ml (1½ pint) pudding basin.

Sieve flour, salt and spice together into a bowl. Stir in breadcrumbs, suet, sugar, chopped walnuts and dates, including rum. Beat eggs and add to pudding mixture with enough milk to make a soft dropping consistency. Turn the pudding mixture into the prepared basin, cover securely and steam for about 2 hours.

Serve hot with a Hard Sauce (see page 157), Vanilla Custard Sauce (see page 29) or thick cream.

Marmalade Pudding

115g (4oz) self-raising flour
Pinch of salt
115g (4oz) suet
115g (4oz) fresh white breadcrumbs
25g (1oz) soft brown sugar
175g (6oz) good-quality dark orange marmalade
Milk, to bind

Serves 4–6

Butter a 1.2 litre (2 pint) pudding basin. Sieve together the flour and salt into a bowl. Add the suet, breadcrumbs and sugar and mix well. Stir the marmalade really well into the dry ingredients, with just enough milk to make a fairly stiff dough. Pour into the prepared basin, cover securely and steam for 2½ hours. Turn out and serve with Vanilla Custard Sauce or Orange Cream Sauce (see pages 29 and 138).

Sweet Sauces to Accompany Puddings

Butterscotch Sauce

60g (2oz) butter

150g (5½oz) demerara sugar

1 tablespoon golden syrup

150g (5½oz) evaporated milk

Melt the butter, then add the sugar and syrup. Stir until dissolved, then pour in the evaporated milk. Turn up the heat and beat until boiling. Serve hot.

Caramel Sauce

150g (5½oz) caster sugar

100ml (3½fl oz) water

200ml (7fl oz) single cream

100g (3½oz) salted butter

Dissolve the sugar in the water in a saucepan. Do not stir. Put the pan on a moderate heat and let it bubble away until it reaches a rich amber colour. Add the cream and take off the heat. Whip in the butter and pour around a baked apple or over ice cream.

If you want it thicker, use double or whipping cream instead of single.

Chocolate Orange Sauce

350ml (12fl oz) water

115g (4oz) caster sugar

1½ tablespoons cornflour

25g (1oz) cocoa powder

1 tablespoon instant coffee granules

50g (1¾oz) good-quality dark chocolate

2 strips of orange zest

Grand Marnier to taste

This easy sauce can be stored in the refrigerator for 4 weeks to use on ice cream or any pudding whenever you fancy. Combine 200ml (7fl oz) water and the sugar in a saucepan. Bring to the boil, stirring occasionally to dissolve the sugar. In a bowl, mix the remaining water with the cornflour and cocoa powder. When the sugar syrup is boiling, stir the cocoa mixture again and then pour it into the pan. Whisk very well, then simmer for 5 minutes. Add the coffee, chocolate and orange zest and stir until smooth. Remove from the heat, cover and leave to cool completely. When the sauce is cold, strain it and flavour to taste with liqueur. Pour the sauce into a jar, cover and store in the refrigerator until needed.

Cider Custard

2 large egg yolks
1 tablespoon cornflour
200ml (7fl oz) cider

2 tablespoons muscovado sugar
¼ teaspoon ground cinnamon
400ml (14fl oz) double cream

In a small basin mix the egg yolks with the cornflour until smooth. Gradually add the cider, the sugar and the cinnamon. Pour into a saucepan and heat gently. Add the cream and whisk constantly over the heat until the custard has thickened.

Coffee Sauce

115g (4oz) demerara sugar
2 tablespoons water

300ml (½ pint) strong black coffee
2 tablespoons Tia Maria

Dissolve the sugar in the water by heating gently in a saucepan. When the sugar has dissolved, boil rapidly until syrup becomes golden. Add coffee and Tia Maria. Boil for a few minutes until syrupy.

Marmalade Sauce

1 level teaspoon cornflour
Juice of 1 orange
300ml (½ pint) white wine

4 heaped tablespoons marmalade
2 tablespoons soft brown sugar

Dissolve cornflour in orange juice. Heat wine, marmalade and sugar in a saucepan until the sugar has dissolved, stirring from time to time. Stir in cornflour mixture and bring to the boil, stirring well. Simmer for 2 minutes. Serve hot.

Chocolate and Coffee Sauce

115g (4oz) good-quality plain
   chocolate, broken into pieces

3 tablespoons strong black coffee
50g (1¾oz) unsalted butter

Put the chocolate and coffee into the top of a double saucepan and stir over the heat until the chocolate has melted. Beat in the butter gradually until the sauce is smooth and glossy.

Creamy Marmalade Sauce

5 rounded tablespoons good-quality
   orange marmalade

2 tablespoons apple juice
150ml (¼ pint) double cream

Put the marmalade in a small saucepan with the apple juice (if the marmalade is very coarse, chop it roughly). Melt it gently over a low heat, stirring from time to time. Pour in the cream and stir carefully until it is thoroughly mixed with the marmalade. Simmer for 3–4 minutes, until slightly thickened. Serve hot.

Hot Brandied Cream

425ml (¾ pint) double cream
40g (1½oz) caster sugar

2–3 tablespoons orange brandy
Grated rind of 1 orange

Put the ingredients into a small pan. Bring to the boil over a low heat, then simmer for 2 minutes. Serve with Christmas pudding.

Orange and Lemon Sauce

15g (½oz) cornflour
300ml (½ pint) full-cream milk
Grated rind and juice of 1 lemon

Grated rind and juice of 1 orange
3 tablespoons golden syrup

Mix cornflour to a paste with 3 tablespoons of the milk. Pour remaining milk into a saucepan and heat gently. Add the lemon and orange rind. Pour hot milk slowly on to cornflour, stirring continuously. Return sauce to pan and simmer for 3 minutes, stirring gently. Stir in fruit juices and golden syrup.

Syrup Sauce

4 tablespoons golden syrup
2 tablespoons water

Juice of ½ lemon

Simmer syrup and water together in a small saucepan for 2–3 minutes. Add lemon juice and serve hot.

Treacle Cream Sauce

4 tablespoons treacle or golden syrup
150ml (¼ pint) single cream

Melt treacle or syrup in a small saucepan. Add cream and heat until almost boiling. Serve hot.

Hard Sauces

Brandy and Lemon Butter

115g (4oz) butter
115g (4oz) caster sugar
½ teaspoon grated lemon rind
1 tablespoon boiling water

1 teaspoon lemon juice
4 tablespoons brandy
Grated lemon rind for decoration

Cut the butter into small pieces and put with sugar and lemon rind in a warmed bowl. Beat until creamy. Add boiling water and continue to beat until every grain of sugar has dissolved (this will prevent sauce from tasting gritty). Add lemon juice and brandy a little at a time, beating continuously to stop sauce curdling. When completely blended, put in an attractive dish and store in refrigerator until needed.

Variations

Add a few chopped glacé cherries and angelica to sauce or a little chopped preserved stem ginger.

Rum and Orange Butter
Make exactly as Brandy and Lemon Butter, substituting orange rind and juice for lemon, and rum for brandy. Serve chilled, sprinkled with grated orange rind.

Senior Wrangler Sauce
Cut the butter into small pieces and put with sugar in a warmed bowl. Beat until creamy. Add ground almonds and boiling water and continue to beat until every grain of sugar has dissolved. Gradually add brandy and almond essence, beating continuously. Serve very cold with rich fruit, steamed and plain sponge puddings.

Index